345

Criminal Law

YOU'VE GOT IT CRACKED

Nutshells – your essential revision and starter guides

- Presents you with the essentials of law in clear and straightforward language, explaining the basic principles

- Incorporates colour to help distinguish cases and legislation and aid ease of use

- Breaks the text down into bite-size chunks and includes bullets where appropriate to aid navigation, assimilation and retention of information

- Opens each chapter with a short introduction to outline the key concepts covered and condense complex and important information

- Closes each chapter with a checklist to enable you to check that all your learning needs have been met

- Provides a model question with answer plan at the end of each chapter to enable you to fully prepare for both exam and essay questions

- Includes diagrams throughout to illustrate difficult concepts

- Places important key definitions and statutory provisions in boxes to help highlight the key points to remember

- Contains a host of useful tools including tables of cases and statutes, a list of examination tips, and a list of useful web resources

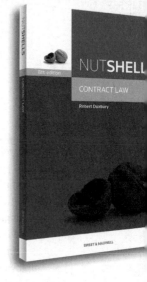

Available from all good booksellers

NUT**CASES**

Criminal Law

SIXTH EDITION

by
PENNY CHILDS
LLB, LLM
Senior Lecturer in Law, University of Plymouth

SWEET & MAXWELL

THOMSON REUTERS

10072123

First Edition – 1996
Second Edition – 1999
Third Edition – 2002
Fourth Edition – 2005
Fifth Edition – 2008

Published in 2011 by Sweet & Maxwell, 100 Avenue Road, London NW3 3PF
part of Thomson Reuters (Professional) UK Limited
(Registered in England & Wales, Company No 1679046.
Registered Office and address for service:
Aldgate House, 33 Aldgate High Street, London EC3N 1DL)

*For further information on our products and services, visit www.sweetandmaxwell.co.uk

Typeset by YHT London
Printed in Great Britain by Ashford Colour Press, Gosport, Hants

*No natural forests were destroyed to make this product;
only farmed timber was used and re-planted.*

A CIP catalogue record for this book is available from the British Library.

ISBN 978-0-414-04618-4

Thomson Reuters and the Thomson Reuters logo are trademarks of Thomson Reuters. Sweet &
Maxwell ® is a registered trademark of Thomson Reuters (Legal) Limited

*Crown copyright material is reproduced with the permission of the Controller of HMSO and the
Queen's Printer for Scotland.*

Contents

Using this Book

Welcome to our new look NUTCASE revision series. We have revamped and improved the existing design and layout and added new features, according to student feedback.

NEW DETAILED TABLE OF CONTENTS for easy navigation.

REDESIGNED TABLES OF CASES AND LEGISLATION for easy reference.

NEW BOXED "THINK POINT"
throughout with further case
analysis and questions
to encourage critical thinking.

THINK POINT

Although an owner of land owns t.
to the heavens, there are statutory
the land. Think about what these a
use of the land.

In addition, other third party ri
owner's use of the land. Consid
be.

...a tests for wheth...
...the two tests set out in *Holland*
...ords in *Elitestone Ltd v Morris* [1997]
...ecided that a bungalow erected on pillars
These cases were also approved in *Che*
(2000) 22 E.G. 147, where it was held that a ho
ropes and connected to utilities was a chatte
nature of the tenancy of a houseboat was
annexation. In *Cinderella Rockerfellas Ltd v Rud*
decided that a vessel which was moored per
of the land for the purpose of assessing its
at it was nonetheless a chattel rather th
for rating purposes.
...ssex Reserve Forces & Cade

NEW COLOUR CODING throughout
to help distinguish cases and
legislation from the narrative.
At the first mention, cases are
highlighted in colour and italicised
and legislation is highlighted in
colour and emboldened.

Table of Cases

Table of Statutes

Actus Reus

. . . .
ACTS AND OMISSIONS

Key Principle
The definition of some offences is restricted to liability for acts. In such cases, an omission is insufficient unless it can be construed as an act.

> FAGAN V METROPOLITAN POLICE COMMISSIONER 1969
> The defendant drove his car onto a policeman's foot. This may have been accidental but he then deliberately refused to move. He claimed that the original act was not assault because he lacked mens rea and the rest of his conduct was an omission which could not amount to assault.

Held
❖ (DC) Defendant's appeal dismissed. Assault cannot be committed by omission. However, the assault was not complete on mounting the foot but continued until the car was removed. Therefore, failing to remove the car was not a mere omission but was part of a continuing act. [1969] 1 Q.B. 439.

Commentary
According to this case, assault is one offence that cannot be committed by pure omission; others include burglary, robbery, attempt and constructive manslaughter. Therefore Fagan would have been acquitted if his conduct could only have been described as an omission. For an alternative way of dealing with assault in this context, see *R. v Santana Bermudez* (2003) (see p.37). For other examples of the consequences and difficulties involved in categorising conduct, see *R. v Miller* (1983) (see p.4) and *Airedale NHS Trust v Bland* (1993) (see p.4).

Key Principle
Where an actus reus can be committed by omission, a defendant who fails to act is only liable if under a duty to act.

Key Principle

A duty to act may arise through contract.

> **R. v INSTAN 1893**
> The defendant lived with her aged aunt who died after the defendant failed to feed her or get medical help when she became unable to care for herself.

Held

❖ (CCCR) Conviction for manslaughter upheld. The defendant was under a duty because food was paid for by the aunt, who relied on the niece as her only source of maintenance. [1893] 1 Q.B. 450.

Commentary

A common law duty can arise from a familial relationship, but it is doubtful whether such a duty arises where the parties are of full age and capacity. It could also arise because the aunt depended on the niece, who had voluntarily assumed a duty (see, for example, *R. v Stone & Dobinson* (1977) at p.3). Moreover, the court felt that the duty could arise from a contract, implied from the circumstances of the case.

> **R. v PITTWOOD 1902**
> A railway gate-keeper, whose duties involved shutting a gate when trains passed, forgot to shut the gate. A person crossing the track was killed by an oncoming train.

Held

❖ (Assize Ct) The defendant was guilty of manslaughter due to the duty imposed by his contract of employment. It did not matter that the contract was between him and a third party (his employers). (1902) 19 T.L.R. 37.

Key Principle

A duty to act may arise from the close relationship between defendant and victim.

> **R. v GIBBINS & PROCTOR 1918**
> A father and his common law wife failed to feed his child who died as a result. They were convicted of murder.

❖ (CA) Defendant's appeal dismissed. The father was guilty of murder, having breached the duty owed by parents to their children. (1918) 13 Cr.App.R. 134.

Commentary

How far this type of duty extends is uncertain. Duties can also be imposed by statute and the duty in this case could today also arise as a statutory duty under the Children and Young Persons Act 1933.

Key Principle

A common law duty to act may arise through the voluntary assumption of care.

R. v STONE & DOBINSON 1977

An aged woman lived with her brother (Stone) and his common law wife (Dobinson). She refused to eat and became seriously ill and bedridden. For a number of reasons, the defendants failed to summon medical help and the sister eventually died.

Held

❖ (CA) Appeal against conviction for manslaughter dismissed. The jury was entitled to decide that the defendants owed a duty to get help or to care for the deceased once she became helplessly infirm. The assumption of a duty could be inferred from the facts that both defendants were aware of her condition; she was a blood relation of Stone, living in his house; and Dobinson had undertaken the duty of trying to wash and feed her. [1977] Q.B. 354.

Commentary

(1) Reference to Stone's relationship with the deceased suggests a common law duty based on special relationship, but it is unlikely that a duty would have been owed if she had not been living in his home. There was no such relationship with Dobinson but she had apparently assumed a duty by trying to care for the deceased. Does this mean that Dobinson would have been under no duty if she had not acted at all? What about Stone?

(2) Other cases falling within this category are *Instan* and the common law wife's duty in *Gibbins & Proctor*.

Key Principle

A common law duty to act may arise from creating a dangerous situation.

> R. v MILLER 1983
>
> The defendant accidentally set fire to a mattress by falling asleep with a lighted cigarette. When he awoke, he failed to take any steps to extinguish the fire or prevent further damage.

Held

❖ (HL) Appeal against conviction for arson dismissed. Arson can be committed by act or omission. Where defendants create a dangerous situation and it is within their power to counteract that danger, a responsibility arises to do so. Since the defendant could, without danger or difficulty, have minimised the risk he had created, his failure to do so amounted to arson. [1983] A.C. 161.

Commentary

(1) The duty is simply to take reasonable steps (safely open to the defendant) and only arose because the defendant created the danger in the first place. Lord Diplock contrasted the case of a passive bystander who sees a fire but is under no duty to act.

(2) The case deals with the Criminal Damage Act 1971 but is of more general application (although it may be restricted to result crimes). For example, in a case on manslaughter, *R. v Evans* (2009) the Court of Appeal held that the defendant who had supplied her half-sister with heroin owed a duty to take reasonable steps by, for example, getting medical help, when she became aware that her sister was exhibiting signs of a heroin overdose. There is a further example of an application of the *Miller* principle in a case of battery in *R. v Santana Bermudez* (2003) (see p.37).

Key Principle

A person may be discharged from their duty to act, incurring no liability for an omission thereafter.

> AIREDALE NHS TRUST v BLAND 1993
>
> A patient had been in a persistent vegetative state for over three years. The doctors and family wanted to withdraw treatment and artificial feeding and the health authority successfully applied for a court order

to do so. The Official Solicitor appealed on the basis that withdrawal breached the doctor's duty to the patient.

Held

❖ (HL) Appeal dismissed. In light of the patient's condition and views of the medical personnel, the declaration was granted. Whilst a doctor was under a duty to act in the best interests of a patient, continuation of treatment was not always in those best interests. In this case, since there was no chance of recovery, withdrawing treatment would not breach the doctor's duty. [1993] A.C. 789.

Commentary

The case further illustrates the difficulties involved in classifying conduct as an act or omission. The court stated that it was always unlawful to take positive steps to end a patient's life. It was only where the case was one of omission that it might be lawful because no duty was breached. This means that liability turns on how the conduct is classified: is withdrawing treatment an act or an omission?

STATES OF AFFAIRS

Key Principle

Conduct must generally be voluntary. However, voluntariness may not be required where the actus reus consists of a state of affairs (or event) rather than conduct.

R. V LARSONNEUR 1933
A Frenchwoman, required to leave the UK, did so by going to Eire. She was deported from Eire and handed to the police in the UK. She was convicted of "being an alien ... found in the UK" (without leave) and appealed on the basis that her return was caused by circumstances over which she had no control.

Held

❖ (CA) Appeal dismissed. The defendant was found in the UK after expiration of permission to be there and so had violated the conditions of her passport. (1933) 24 Cr.App.R. 74.

Commentary

The case has been criticised since the defendant's presence was involuntary. However, the cause of the prohibited state of affairs was apparently irrelevant. A similar decision was reached in *Winzar* (1983), where the defendant was guilty of "being found drunk … on a highway", having been placed there by the police.

UNLAWFULNESS

Key Principle

The word "unlawful" may be included as part of the actus reus of a crime.

> R. v WILLIAMS (GLADSTONE) 1984
>
> The defendant punched the victim mistakenly believing that the victim was unlawfully assaulting another. He was convicted of assault occasioning actual bodily harm and appealed against the direction that his honest belief that he was acting lawfully was only relevant if based on reasonable grounds. Whether this was a misdirection depended on whether the word "unlawful" was a matter of defence or part of the actus reus of the offence (see Ch.2).

Held

❖ (CA) Appeal allowed for reasons explained in Ch.2. The word "unlawful" was part of the actus reus of assault, with the prosecution bearing the burden of proving that the actions were unlawful. Therefore the defendant had made a mistake about an element appearing in the actus reus of the crime charged. (1984) 78 Cr.App.R. 276.

Commentary

This decision was further approved by the Privy Council in *Beckford v R.* (1988) (see Ch.14 p.168).

CAUSATION—IN FACT

Key Principle

Causation in fact requires that the defendant's conduct be a sine qua non ("but-for" cause) of a result.

> R. v WHITE 1910
>
> The defendant was charged with murder having put cyanide into his mother's drink with the intention to kill her. Medical evidence established that her death was due to heart failure and not the poison.

Held

❖ (CA) The defendant was not guilty of murder, but he was, on the evidence, guilty of attempted murder. [1910] 2 K.B. 124.

Commentary

Whilst the decision (concerned with attempted murder) does not deal directly with the point, it is a good illustration of lack of factual causation. But for his act, the defendant's mother would still have died and so he was not the sine qua non (cause) of her death.

CAUSATION—IN LAW

Key Principle

The defendant's conduct does not have to be the sole (or main) cause of a result but it must more than minimally contribute to it.

> **R. v Pagett 1983**
> The defendant held a woman in front of him as he fired at armed police. The police returned fire, killing the woman. The defendant appealed against conviction on two grounds:
> (1) the immediate cause of the death was the act of the police and not attributable to the defendant.
> (2) the judge had misdirected the jury in saying that causation was matter of law rather than fact.

Held

❖ (CA) Appeal dismissed.

(1) The defendant had caused the death despite the actions of the police. A defendant "need not be the sole cause or even the main cause ... it being enough that his act contributed significantly".

(2) Causation is a question for the jury to decide on the facts but must be decided in accordance with legal principles. (1983) 76 Cr.App.R. 279.

Key Principle

If an event intervenes between the defendant's conduct and the result, it may be a novus actus interveniens (a new operative cause), breaking the chain of causation.

R. v Jordan 1956

The defendant stabbed the victim who died a few days later following treatment for the wound. The wound had almost healed and the immediate cause of death was the medical treatment, described as "palpably wrong". The defendant appealed against conviction for murder.

Held

❖ (CA) Conviction quashed. The direct and immediate cause of death was a separate and independent feature (the treatment) and not the stab wound. (1956) 40 Cr.App.R. 152.

Commentary

It was suggested that where death arose from normal treatment for an injury, the injury could be said to be a cause of death. However, this treatment was not normal and so broke the chain. A further example of the key principle can be found in *R. v Rafferty* (2007) where the defendant was involved with two other defendants in assaulting the victim. When the defendant left, the remaining two defendants drowned the victim in the sea. This amounted to a novus actus interveniens preventing the defendant from being a cause of the victim's death.

Key Principle

An intervening event will not break the chain of causation if the defendant's conduct is still an operative and substantial cause of the result.

R. v Smith 1959

The defendant stabbed the victim, causing internal injury. A medical officer, not realising the nature of the injury, gave "thoroughly bad" treatment. The victim died within two hours of being stabbed but might not have died if given different treatment. The defendant appealed against conviction for murder on the basis that the treatment broke the chain.

Held

❖ (CMAC) Appeal dismissed. Death resulted from the original wound which was still an operating and substantial cause of the death despite other operative causes. [1959] 2 Q.B. 35.

Commentary

The court distinguished *Jordan* as "a very particular case, depending on its exact facts". *Jordan* was also said to be "very exceptional" (and *Smith* was preferred) in *Malcherek & Steel* (1981) (CA) where life support for two injured victims was disconnected by doctors. Since the treatment was "normal and conventional" and the original injuries were still operative, the court held that discontinuing treatment did not break the chain of causation. Also, note the view in *Airedale* that allowing a patient to die of a pre-existing condition does not, in law, amount to causing the death which is still treated as caused by the pre-existing condition. Overall, the distinction between *Smith* and *Jordan* seems to be that in *Jordan* the wound, having practically healed, ceased to operate. Any attempt to distinguish the cases on the degree of fault involved in the treatment should now be avoided according to *R. v Cheshire* (1991) (see below).

Key Principle

To operate as a novus actus interveniens, the intervening event must be so potent and independent of the defendant's actions as to render those actions "insignificant".

> **R. v Cheshire 1991**
> The defendant shot the victim in the abdomen and thigh. The victim developed breathing difficulties, necessitating a tracheotomy. Two months after the shooting, the wounds had practically healed but the victim died from complications caused by the tracheotomy. The defendant was convicted of murder and appealed against the direction that only grossly negligent or reckless treatment broke the chain of causation.

Held

❖ (CA) Appeal dismissed. It was a misdirection to focus on the degree of fault involved in the medical treatment but no miscarriage of justice had occurred. The complication from which the victim died was a direct consequence of the defendant's conduct which was still a significant cause of the death. This was not an extraordinary or unusual case where treatment was so independent of the defendant's conduct and so potent in causing death as to exonerate the defendant. [1991] 3 All E.R. 670.

Commentary

(1) Factually, the case is similar to *Jordan* since the original wound had ceased to operate. However, only treatment that is so extraordinary as to be independent of the defendant's conduct breaks the chain and obiter in *Cheshire* suggests that incompetence does not of itself render treatment "abnormal in the sense of extraordinary".

(2) Consider whether this principle (and those below relating to intervening acts of the victim) might assist the prosecution in proving causation where the victim commits suicide as a result of the defendant's actions. See, for example, the comments made obiter in *R. v Dhaliwal* (2006) where a woman committed suicide whilst suffering from psychological damage caused by prolonged spousal abuse.

Key Principle

A free, deliberate and informed intervention will break the chain of causation.

> R v KENNEDY 2007
>
> The defendant prepared a syringe of heroin and presented it ready for use to the deceased, who, acting freely and voluntarily, used it to inject himself and died as a result. The defendant appealed against his conviction for manslaughter.

Held

❖ (HL) Defendant's conviction quashed. The deceased's act of self-injection, being informed, deliberate and voluntary, broke the chain of causation.

Commentary

In *Environment Agency v Empress Car Co (Abertillery) Ltd* (1999) (HL) a company was found guilty of causing pollution when a tap on their oil tank was opened by an unknown third party and so discharged oil into a river. It was held that this act did not break the chain because it was foreseeable. In *Kennedy* the House of Lords approved but distinguished this earlier decision, stressing that the principles of causation may differ according to the context.

Key Principle

An intervening act will not break the chain of causation if it is dependent on the defendant's conduct and not a free (voluntary) act.

R. v Pagett 1983
(see p.7).

Held

❖ (CA) In dismissing the defendant's appeal, the court stated that an intervention must be independent and voluntary ("free, deliberate and informed") to break the chain. A reasonable act of self-defence or self-preservation (such as the police returning fire) did not break the chain because it was an involuntary response, dependent on the defendant's actions. For the same reason, an act carried out in the execution of a legal duty (such as preventing a crime or effecting an arrest) would not operate as a novus actus. (1983) 76 Cr.App.R. 279.

Key Principle

An attempt by the victim to escape from the defendant's conduct will not break the chain of causation if it is reasonably foreseeable.

R. v Williams & Davis 1992
A hitch-hiker jumped from a moving car and died from the injuries sustained. The victim had, according to the prosecution, jumped to escape violence from the defendants who intended to rob him.

Held

❖ (CA) Appeal against conviction for manslaughter allowed. An attempt to escape from a threat does not break the chain if it is within the range of responses which could be foreseen by the reasonable person. However, in this case, there was insufficient evidence about the nature of the threat to determine whether or not the hitch-hiker's response was reasonable. [1992] 2 All E.R. 183.

Commentary

The case confirms the conditions applying to escape attempts: the defendant caused the victim immediate fear of being hurt; the fear was well-founded and caused the escape attempt in the course of which the injury was sustained; the response was a natural consequence of the defendant's action (i.e. reasonably foreseeable as likely to happen, bearing in mind the agony of the moment and any particular characteristics of the victim). Compare the decision with *R. v Roberts* (1971) (see Ch.4 p.44) where there was sufficient evidence to suggest that the victim's response was reasonably foreseeable rather than "daft" or unexpected.

Key Principle

An "abnormality" in the victim will not break the chain of causation, even if it is not reasonably foreseeable.

> **R. v BLAUE 1975**
> The defendant stabbed the victim who died after refusing a blood transfusion because she was a Jehovah's witness. The defendant appealed against conviction for manslaughter on the basis that the victim's refusal broke the chain.

Held

❖ (CA) Appeal dismissed. The operative cause of the victim's death was the stab wound and not her refusal of treatment. The chain was not broken by the refusal because "people must take their victims as they find them". [1975] 3 All E.R. 446.

Commentary

The rule, stated obiter, that victims be taken as found (which covers physical and other attributes) prevents a break in the chain even though it may be an unforeseeable "abnormality". However this principle will not mean that a defendant is always liable where the prohibited result is caused by an "abnormality" in the victim because the other elements of the offence charged must also be proved. See, for example, *R. v Carey, Coyle, Foster* (2006) where an undiagnosed heart disease contributed to the death of a 15-year-old victim and *R. v Dawson* (1985) at p.65.

Key Principle

If the defendant commits a number of different acts and the prosecution cannot prove which one caused the specified result, the defendant must be acquitted unless mens rea accompanied each of the acts that may have caused the result.

> **ATTORNEY-GENERAL'S REFERENCE (NO.4 OF 1980) 1981**
> The defendant slapped the victim, causing her to fall downstairs and bang her head. He dragged her upstairs by a piece of rope tied around her neck, cut her throat, dismembered her body and disposed of the pieces. The prosecution could not prove which act caused her death and the judge directed an acquittal.

❖ (CA) It was not necessary to prove which act caused death as long as the jury was satisfied that each possible cause was accompanied by the relevant mens rea. However, if the jury felt that any one of the relevant acts was not accompanied by mens rea, they must acquit even where satisfied that the remaining acts were so accompanied. [1981] 2 All E.R. 617.

Commentary

A conviction for manslaughter was possible because evidence suggested that all of the acts were accompanied by the mens rea of manslaughter. Contrast *Fisher* (1987) (CA), where the prosecution could not prove whether death was caused by hitting the victim or by dragging him downstairs. The defendant was acquitted because whilst the dragging was accompanied by mens rea, the blow may have been in self-defence.

CONTEMPORANEITY

Key Principle

The actus reus and mens rea of a crime must be contemporaneous (coincide in time). Where an actus reus initially occurs without mens rea, contemporaneity may be achieved if the actus reus is construed as a continuing act and mens rea occurs during its continuance.

> FAGAN V METROPOLITAN POLICE COMMISSIONER 1969.
> (see p.1).

Held

❖ (DC) Appeal dismissed. The court confirmed that "… both … actus reus and mens rea must be present at the same time". However, lack of contemporaneity was avoided by construing the actus reus as continuing from its inception (when there was no mens rea) until the car was removed (when there was mens rea). [1969] 1 Q.B. 439.

Commentary

For another illustration of this principle, see *Kaitamaki v R.* (1985) (Ch.5, p.49). A similar problem arose in *Miller* (1983) where the act of starting the fire was not accompanied by mens rea. Mens rea was formed later when the defendant failed to act. The Court of Appeal adopted the approach in *Fagan*, treating the conduct as a continuing act so that mens rea was formed during its continuance. The House of Lords rejected this approach, deciding that the conduct was an omission and not a continuing act. They achieved the same result by holding that the failure to act (accompanied by mens rea) was the actus reus. This approach is only possible where the offence can be committed by omission and there is a duty to act.

Key Principle

Where a series of acts culminates in the actus reus, and mens rea existed before but not at the time of the actus reus, contemporaneity is achieved if the series of acts is a continuous transaction connecting actus reus and mens rea.

> THABO MELI V R. 1954
> In pursuance of a pre-conceived plan to kill and evade detection, the defendants assaulted the victim. Believing him to be dead, they "staged" an accident by dropping the body over a cliff where the victim ultimately died from exposure.

Held

❖ (PC) Defendant's appeal against conviction for murder dismissed. The first act(s), done with mens rea, did not cause death and the act(s) which did cause death were not accompanied by mens rea. However, the acts were not separate. They were all part of the plan and therefore represented one series of acts during which actus reus and mens rea were present. [1954] 1 All E.R. 373.

> R. V CHURCH 1966
> The defendant was convicted of manslaughter, having assaulted the victim with intent. Apparently believing the victim to be dead, he threw her body in a river where she died from drowning.

Held

❖ (CA) Defendant's appeal dismissed. The jury was entitled to treat the series of acts as one course of conduct. Therefore, because the first act would establish (at least) manslaughter if the victim had died, the defendant was guilty even though he lacked mens rea at the time of doing the act that caused death. [1966] 1 Q.B. 59.

Commentary

(1) The court also felt that murder was possible if the series of acts was designed to cause death or grievous bodily harm.

(2) There was no pre-conceived plan as in *Thabo Meli* (1954) nor did the court explain why, in the absence of such, this could still be viewed as one transaction. Explanation comes in the next case.

> ## R. v LE BRUN 1992
> In the course of an argument, the defendant hit his wife, causing her to become unconscious. In dragging her away thereafter, he caused her death by accidentally dropping her body. He was convicted of manslaughter.

Held

❖ (CA) Defendant's appeal dismissed. Where there is a time interval between the act done with mens rea (the original assault) and the act that causes death, there may still be a conviction if all the acts are part of the same sequence of events (the same transaction). This is easily established where the subsequent actions are designed to conceal the original act done with mens rea. [1992] Q.B. 61.

Commentary

(1) The court distinguished *Thabo Meli* (1954) because there was no pre-conceived plan. Moreover, unlike *Thabo Meli* or *Church*, the defendant did not believe he was disposing of a corpse.

(2) The continuous transaction principle dealt with lack of contemporaneity. Even if the second act was the sole cause of the death, liability arose because it was part of the same transaction as the act accompanied by mens rea. The court approved a distinction between subsequent acts by which the defendant was trying to assist the victim (such as trying to get the body to hospital) and acts not so designed (such as disposal or trying to conceal the original act). The latter established the continuous transaction whilst the former might not.

(3) The case also raises an issue of causation. If the first act is a contributory cause of the death and accompanied by mens rea, there is no difficulty with contemporaneity and the defendant is guilty because his subsequent acts do not operate as a novus actus interveniens. Acts designed to evade liability do not break the chain linking the original act to the death, but acts designed to assist the victim might.

THINK POINT

In *R. v Evans* (2009) (see p.4) the defendant was said to have committed the *actus reus* of manslaughter on the basis of her failure to act when under a duty to do so. Can you explain why she could not be said to have committed the *actus reus* of manslaughter by supplying the heroin to the victim in the first place? Is there any potential conflict between the decision in this case that the supply created or contributed to the danger of death and the decision in *R. v Kennedy* (2007)?

In *R. v Dhaliwal* (2006) a woman committed suicide due to psychological damage which had been caused by being subjected to prolonged domestic abuse by her husband. Consider the ways in which it might be possible to argue that her actions did not break the chain of causation so that her husband would remain responsible for causing her death.

Mens Rea

....

2

INTENTION

Key Principle
Aim, purpose or desire is a type of intention.

> **R. v STEANE 1947**
> The defendant was convicted of doing acts likely to assist the enemy with intent to do so, having made war-time broadcasts for the Germans. He appealed on the basis that he acted in order to save his family and not to assist the enemy.

Held
❖ (CA) Appeal allowed. The defendant's actions were consistent with the innocent intention claimed rather than the criminal intent charged because he had acted with the desire of saving his family from a concentration camp. [1947] K.B. 997.

Commentary
The court recognised that motive and intention are different concepts, but the decision seems not only to equate the two but also to restrict the meaning of intention to desire.

Key Principle
A result can be intended even though not desired (or wanted).

> **R. v MOLONEY 1985**
> (see p.18).

Commentary
In explaining the distinction between intention and motive or desire, Lord Bridge gave an example of a man boarding a plane he knew to be bound for Manchester. Although his aim (motive/desire) was to escape pursuit and he might not actually "want" to go to Manchester, he did, in law, intend to go

there because he knew that he was "morally certain" to arrive there. This recognises that intent has a wider meaning than that given in *Steane*.

Key Principle

A jury may infer intention from the defendant's foresight of consequences.

> **R. v MOLONEY 1985**
> A soldier shot and killed his stepfather in response to a drunken challenge. He claimed that he had not aimed the gun at the victim and had, at the time, no idea that firing it would cause injury. The judge directed that intention included both desire and foresight of probable consequences and the defendant was convicted of murder.

Held

❖ (HL) Appeal allowed, manslaughter substituted.

(1) The jury was not directed on the defence that the risk of injury had not crossed the defendant's mind at the time.

(2) The mens rea of murder (intention to kill or cause grievous bodily harm) should normally be left to the jury without explanation. However, in rare cases, judges should direct that intention might be inferred if the consequence was foreseen as a natural one by the defendant. Such knowledge or foresight was not equivalent to intention but was, at most, evidence of intention. [1985] A.C. 905.

Commentary

(1) The House of Lords confirmed that Criminal Justice Act 1961, s.8 abolished the presumption that a person intends the "natural and probable consequences" of their actions. A jury is not bound to infer intention from this alone but must consider all of the evidence.

(2) The case also establishes that intention differs from desire and from foresight of consequences. The latter is simply evidence of intent. Lord Bridge gave five examples of the requisite degree of foresight which referred to levels of high probability. However, his model direction simply referred to "natural consequences". This caused controversy because of ambiguity in the meaning of "natural consequence". In *R. v Hancock & Shankland* (1986) the House of Lords reaffirmed that foresight of consequences was no more than evidence of intention. However, the House declared the *Moloney*

guidelines were unsatisfactory because they omitted reference to probability. In addition to the guidelines, a jury should be directed that the greater the probability of a consequence, the more likely that it was foreseen and therefore also intended. This refines the *Moloney* direction but both cases must now be considered in the light of *R. v Woollin* (below).

Key Principle

Intention may be established where a consequence is a virtual certainty and the defendant realised that it was a virtual certainty.

> R. V WOOLLIN 1998
>
> The defendant killed his child by throwing him onto a hard surface. Part of the judge's direction suggested that intention could be established if he realised that there was a substantial risk of grievous bodily harm.

Held

❖ (HL) Appeal allowed, manslaughter substituted for murder. Using the phrase "substantial risk" was a misdirection, blurring the distinction between intention and recklessness. The direction from *R. v Nedrick* (1986) (CA) was approved. This direction had been that a jury is not entitled to infer intent unless the defendant appreciated that the consequence was a virtual certainty. [1998] 4 All E.R. 103.

Commentary

(1) It seems that the prosecution has to prove that the result is actually virtually certain and not simply that the defendant believes it to be virtually certain: *R. v Matthews & Alleyne* (2003) (CA).

(2) It is confirmed by the Court of Appeal in *R. v MD* (2004) that the consequence does not have to be virtually certain in cases of purposive intent and that the *Woollin* direction should only be given in "rare circumstances" where the defendant has acted without the purpose of bringing about the result.

(3) Whilst confirming the *Nedrick* direction, the House of Lords in *Woollin* replaced the word "infer" (used in the *Nedrick* direction) with the word "find". This change in terminology led to the suggestion that the case might have changed the law as stated in *Moloney*, so that foresight of virtual certainty was now proof of intent rather than just evidence of it. However, the case also contains statements that support the view that foresight of virtual

certainty remains evidence of intent. This view is confirmed by the Court of Appeal in *R. v Matthews & Alleyne*.

RECKLESSNESS

Key Principle

Recklessness involves unreasonable risk-taking where the defendant is aware of the existence of the risk being taken.

> R. v G 2003
>
> Two boys, aged 11 and 12, went camping without their parents' permission. They lit some newspaper in the back yard of a shop and threw it under a large plastic wheelie-bin. They left without putting out the fire. The fire spread to the shop causing over £1,000,000 worth of damage. The boys had expected the lighted newspaper to burn itself out and had not appreciated any risk of the fire spreading in the way it did. They were convicted of arson contrary to s.1 of the **Criminal Damage Act 1971** following a direction based on the definition of recklessness laid down in *R. v Caldwell* (see below). The Court of Appeal dismissed their appeal.

Held

❖ (HL) Defendants' appeal allowed. "A person acts . . . 'recklessly' [within the meaning of s.1 of the **1971 Act**] with respect to:

(i) a circumstance when he is aware of a risk that it exists or will exist;

(ii) a result when he is aware of a risk that it will occur; and it is, in the circumstances known to him, unreasonable to take the risk . . ." [2003] 4 All E.R. 765.

Commentary

(1) The definition of recklessness given in this case is based on that given in cl.18(c) of the Draft Criminal Code 1989 and confirms the test for recklessness established in *R. v Cunningham* (1957). In that case, the defendant had broken into a gas meter in order to steal the contents. Gas had escaped, partially suffocating the victim. The defendant's conviction for maliciously administering a noxious thing was quashed by the Court of Appeal because of a misdirection that "maliciously" meant "wickedly". The court held that the word "maliciously" required proof that the defendant either intended the result (administration of a noxious substance) or was reckless in the sense that he foresaw that result might be caused but nevertheless went on to take that risk.

(2) This subjective test of advertent recklessness means that those incapable of appreciating risks are not reckless. Thus in *R. v Stephenson* (1979), the defendant's conviction for reckless arson was quashed because he may not have appreciated or considered the risk of damage due to schizophrenia.

(3) According to the Court of Appeal in *R. v Brady* (2006) the decision in *R. v G* does not require that the defendant foresees the risk as "an obvious and significant risk"; foreseeing any degree of risk is sufficient.

Key Principle

A defendant is not reckless where s/he fails to give thought to the existence of the risk being taken, even though that risk may have been an obvious and serious one.

> R. v G 2003
> (see above).

Commentary

(1) In this case the House of Lords decided that only advertent risk-taking amounts to recklessness. Inadvertent risk-taking is no longer sufficient. In so doing, the House of Lords overruled its earlier decision in the case of *R. v Caldwell* (1982). In *R. v Caldwell*, the defendant set fire to a hotel and claimed to have been so drunk that the risk of endangering lives had not crossed his mind. In deciding that self-induced intoxication was not relevant to the charge under s.1(2) of the **Criminal Damage Act 1971** (see Ch.13), Lord Diplock defined recklessness as including not only recognising a risk and going on to take it, but also failing to give any thought to whether there is a risk when, if thought were given, it would be obvious that there was. The House of Lords in *R. v G* concluded that the earlier case had "misconstrued s.1 of the Act" and was "offensive to principle and ... apt to cause injustice". This was due in part to the fact that the test applied to determine whether a defendant was inadvertently reckless was whether the risk in question would be obvious to a reasonable person. This had led to the conviction of defendants such as the 14-year-old girl in *Elliott v C (A Minor)* (1983). She had set fire to white spirit which had then destroyed a shed. She had given no thought to the risk and even if she had done so, it was established that the risk would not have been obvious to her. The test applied, with regret, by the Divisional Court was whether the risk would have been obvious to a reasonable person.

(2) The House of Lords rejected the invitation to impose liability for

inadvertent recklessness where the risk would have been obvious to the defendant if thought had been given. Their Lordships also rejected the possibility of liability arising where the risk would have been obvious to the reasonable person in the defendant's situation. Liability simply does not now arise for inadvertent risk taking.

(3) Their Lordships made it clear that they were only considering the meaning of reckless in the context of s.1 of the **Criminal Damage Act 1971**. However, prior to this case, the *Caldwell* test for inadvertent recklessness had been rejected in a number of areas: rape: *R. v Satnam and Kewal* (1983); manslaughter: *R. v Adomako* (1995); and crimes of malice: *R. v Savage and Parmenter* (1992). Therefore it seems likely that *R. v G* provides a definition of recklessness of universal application and this opinion is expressed in *R. v Brady* (2006), a case involving s.20 of the Offences Against the Person Act 1861.

Key Principle

A defendant who considers whether a risk exists and genuinely decides that there is no risk is not reckless.

CHIEF CONSTABLE OF AVON AND SOMERSET V SHIMMEN 1987

An expert in Korean self-defence was charged with criminal damage having unintentionally broken a window. The court accepted that he was not reckless because, relying on his skill, he had decided that the window would not break.

Held

❖ (DC) Prosecution appeal allowed. Defendants are not reckless if they consider the risk and decide that there is none. However, this defendant had realised that there was some risk but had thought that he could avoid it. Thus he was reckless in the sense of realising a risk and going on to take it. (1987) 84 Cr.App.R. 7 Q.B.D.

Commentary

Defendants who consider a risk and decide that there is none do not fall within advertent recklessness because they have not decided to run the risk. This is really no more than an application of the general principle laid down in *DPP v Morgan* (1976) (see p.24) and confirmed in *B (A Child) v DPP* (2000) (see p.25) that a genuine mistake of fact negates mens rea.

TRANSFERRED MALICE

Key Principle

If the defendant has the mens rea of a crime and causes the actus reus of that crime against an unforeseen victim, the original mens rea is transferred to the actual actus reus.

> **R. v LATIMER 1886**
> The defendant intended to strike a man but accidentally struck the woman standing next to him. He was convicted under **Offences Against the Person Act 1861** S.20.

Held

❖ (CCCR) Defendant's appeal dismissed. The defendant was guilty because "if a person has a malicious intent towards one person, and in carrying into effect that malicious intent he injures another ... he is guilty of what the law considers malice against the person so injured." (1886) 17 Q.B.D. 359.

Commentary

The principle applies equally to offences against property. The House of Lords in *Attorney-General's Reference (No.3 of 1994)* (1998) (see p.58) confirmed the existence of the principle although it was deemed to be a fiction without "any sound intellectual basis". On the particular facts of the case, the court refused to apply the principle because of a lack of compatibility between the intent directed at the mother (intent to cause grievous bodily harm) and the result inflicted on the child (death) and because it would have involved a "double transfer" of intent from the mother to the foetus and from the foetus to the child.

Key Principle

Malice can only be transferred if the actus reus (for which there is mens rea) is the same as the actus reus actually committed.

> **R. v PEMBLITON 1874**
> The defendant aimed a stone at a group of people but it broke a window instead and he was found guilty of criminal damage.

Held

❖ (CCCR) Conviction quashed. Since there was no finding that the defendant was reckless about breaking the window, the intent to strike a person could not provide the mens rea for maliciously injuring property. (1872-75) L.R. 2 C.C.R. 119.

Commentary

In *Attorney-General's Reference (No.3 of 1994)* (1998) (see p.58), it was said that the principle only applies where the intention is to do a particular kind of harm and that kind of harm is then actually done. This would restrict the principle because it means that the mens rea of some crimes (for example, intention to cause grievous bodily harm in murder) cannot be transferred to the actus reus (killing) because it is not the same kind of harm.

MISTAKE OF FACT

Key Principle

A genuine mistake about the existence of a definitional (actus reus) element of a crime negates mens rea whether or not that mistake is based on reasonable grounds.

> DPP v MORGAN 1976
>
> The defendants were convicted of rape although they claimed a mistaken belief that the woman was consenting. They appealed against the direction that they were only entitled to rely on their belief if it was both honestly and reasonably held.

Held

❖ (HL) Appeal dismissed. There was a misdirection but no miscarriage of justice. The mens rea of rape is intention to have intercourse without consent or recklessness, not caring whether there is lack of consent. An honest belief in consent negatives that mens rea. The mistake does not also have to be reasonable. [1976] A.C. 182.

Commentary

(1) The mistake is not a "defence" but simply denies the prosecution case. Whilst the mistake does not have to be reasonable, lack of reasonable grounds may be evidence that the belief was not genuinely held. This was the reason for dismissing the appeal.

(2) The court distinguished *Tolson* (1889) (see p.26) and *Prince* (1875) (see p.26) as cases dealing with offences that do not require proof of mens rea. Cases of defences were also distinguished. Thus, much turns on whether the mistake relates to a "definitional" (actus reus) element or a defence element.

The same reasoning was used in *Williams* (1984) (see Ch.1, p.6) where the word "unlawful" was held to be part of the actus reus of assault. Therefore even an unreasonable mistake about the lawfulness of the act negated mens rea. This was confirmed in *Beckford* (1988) (see Ch.14, p.168).

(3) Under the Sexual Offences Act 2003, the law relating to rape has been changed. Rape is now committed unless the defendant reasonably believes that the complainant consents. This would affect the decision in *Morgan* in so far as it deals with rape, but it does not affect the general principle laid down in the case.

> B (A CHILD) V DIRECTOR OF PUBLIC PROSECUTIONS 2000
> The defendant, a 15-year-old boy, was charged with inciting a girl under the age of 14 to commit an act of gross indecency contrary to s.1 of the Indecency With Children Act 1960. Although the defendant honestly believed the girl to be over the age of 14, he was convicted on the basis that the age element in the offence was one of strict liability.

Held
❖ (HL) Defendant's appeal allowed. Section 1(1) of the **Indecency With Children Act 1960** did not create a strict liability offence. A defendant was entitled to an acquittal if he held the honest belief that the child was aged 14 or over. The belief did not have to be based on reasonable grounds. [2000] 2 A.C. 428.

Commentary
(1) The House of Lords in *R. v K* (2001) reached a similar decision in relation to a charge of indecently assaulting a girl under the age of 16. Note that the law in both of these areas has been changed by the **Sexual Offences Act 2003**. However this does not affect the general principle represented by the above case law.

(2) The case confirms that the *Morgan* principle is one of general application to offences that require proof of mens rea and that it represents a common law principle that is to be preferred to that laid down in *R. v Tolson* (see p.26). The case also confirms that the burden of proof is on the prosecution to establish lack of honest belief.

Key Principle

A mistake about the existence of a definitional (actus reus) element of a crime is irrelevant (even where genuine and reasonable) if the element is one of strict liability and not afforded a defence of mistake.

R. v PRINCE 1875

The defendant was convicted of abducting a girl under the age of 16. He appealed on the basis that he reasonably believed that she was aged 18.

Held

❖ (CCCR) Appeal dismissed. The statute did not specify mens rea in respect of the age. That element was therefore one of strict liability and since the girl was, in fact, under the age of 16 the defendant was guilty. [1874-80] All E.R. 881.

Commentary

(1) The court distinguished other elements of the offence for which mens rea was required and where mistake might excuse the defendant.

(2) Not only did the statute not provide for mens rea in respect of "age" but it also provided no defence. Contrast *Tolson* (see below).

(3) Prior to the passing of the **Sexual Offences Act 2003**, the decision in *B (A Child) v DPP* (2000) (see above and Ch.3, p.28) overruled the decision in *R. v Prince* in so far as it dealt with abduction. However, this did not affect the general principle and mistakes about strict liability elements are still irrelevant.

Key Principle

In some cases, a mistake about the existence of a definitional (actus reus) element of a crime, which need not be accompanied by mens rea, may excuse if based on reasonable grounds.

R. v TOLSON 1889

The defendant was convicted of bigamy. She remarried whilst her first husband was alive, genuinely and reasonably believing that he was dead.

Held

❖ (CCCR) Defendant's appeal allowed. The relevant statute did not require proof of mens rea in respect of "being married". However, it did not exclude (either expressly or implicitly) a defence of honest and reasonable belief that the first husband was dead. The defendant, who honestly and reasonably believed that she was no longer married, was not guilty of bigamy. (1889) L.R. 23 Q.B.D. 168.

Commentary

The court distinguished *Prince* (1875) where the policy behind the offence was such that there was no defence of reasonable mistake. It had been suggested that *Tolson* created a general (objective) principle that mistaken belief had to be both honest and reasonable to exonerate a defendant. This is rejected in *B (A Child) v DPP* (2000) (see p.25 and Ch.3, p.28). The principle of general application is now that of (subjective) honest belief. This may mean that the decision in relation to bigamy in *Tolson* is incorrect. Alternatively it may be that bigamy is an exception to the general principle being, in effect, an example of a crime of negligence rather than mens rea. A mistake about an element satisfied by negligence would still need to be based on reasonable grounds.

THINK POINT

Look back at the decisions of *R. v Woollin* (1998) at p.19 and *R. v G* (2003) at p.20. According to the decisions in these two cases, what is the difference between intention and recklessness? It might help to consider the following scenario. How would you classify the defendant's state of mind when she deliberately sets fire to a house knowing that there are people inside who are likely to get injured in the fire? Does she intend them to get injured? Is she reckless about them getting injured?

The House of Lords in *R. v G* (2003) (see p.20) overruled *R. v Caldwell* (1982) (see p.21) on the basis that it was "offensive to principle......and apt to cause injustice" What principle were they referring to? Do you agree that the *Caldwell* test caused 'injustice' and can you explain why? What about the new test—is it any better or does it, too, cause potential injustice? It might help to consider arguments in favour of including inadvertence within the definition of recklessness but only where the defendant could have appreciated the risk if s/he had thought about it.

Strict Liability

3

Key Principle

Where a statute does not refer to a state of mind, there is a presumption in favour of mens rea.

> B (A Child) v Director of Public Prosecutions 2000
> (see p.25).

Held

❖ (HL) Defendant's appeal allowed. Section 1(1) of the **Indecency With Children Act 1960** did not create a strict liability offence and the prosecution was required to prove mens rea. Where a statute makes no reference to mens rea "the starting point for a court is the established common law presumption that a mental element, traditionally labelled mens rea, is an essential ingredient ..." per Lord Nicholls. [2000] 2 A.C. 428.

Commentary

Lord Steyn refers to the presumption as an element of the "principle of legality" under which Parliament is assumed to have legislated. Judgments in the cases of *Sweet v Parsley* (1970) (see p.29) and *Gammon Ltd v Attorney-General of Hong Kong* (1985) (see p.33) were cited with approval. In the former, Lord Reid said "... whenever a section is silent as to mens rea, there is a presumption that ... we must read in words appropriate to require mens rea". In the latter, the Privy Council listed a number of factors to be considered in determining whether an offence was one of strict liability. The first was that "there is a presumption of law that mens rea is required".

Key Principle

The presumption in favour of mens rea can only be displaced by necessary implication.

> B (A Child) v Director of Public Prosecutions 2000
> (see above).

Their Lordships made clear that if Parliament had not expressly excluded mens rea, strict liability should not be imposed just because it was reasonable to infer that it was intended. The need for mens rea could only be negatived by necessary implication which "connotes an implication which is compellingly clear". Factors that might be taken into account in deciding whether there was such an implication included "the language used, the nature of the offence, the mischief sought to be prevented and any other circumstances which may assist..." per Lord Nicholls.

Key Principle

In determining whether strict liability is a necessary implication, the court will consider the statutory words used in describing the offence.

> ALPHACELL V WOODWARD 1972
>
> Pumps failed to work properly which caused polluted water to overflow from the defendant's tanks. The company was convicted of "causing" pollution and appealed on the basis that the offence required proof of mens rea.

Held

❖ (HL) Appeal dismissed. The word "cause" was not accompanied by mens rea words and did not in itself imply mens rea. It was a strict liability offence. [1972] A.C. 824.

Commentary

Other statutory words have also been held to create strict liability. For example, "using" (as in using a vehicle in contravention of regulations: *James & Son v Smee* (1955)) and "possession" (see *Warner v Metropolitan Police Commissioner* (1969) below). Other words import mens rea, such as "permitting", "allowing", and "suffering". Even "causing" in a different context from that in *Alphacell* has been held to import mens rea: *James & Son v Smee* (1955) (causing another to contravene the regulations). The next case is another illustration of a word interpreted as importing mens rea.

> SWEET V PARSLEY 1970
>
> A landlady was charged with being concerned in the management of premises, used for the purpose of smoking cannabis. She occasionally visited the premises but was unaware of the cannabis smoking. She was convicted on the basis of strict liability.

Held ....

❖ (HL) Defendant's appeal allowed. The offence was not one of strict liability. Considering the words of the statute in question, the House decided that it must be the manager's purpose (intention) that the premises be used for the smoking of cannabis or, at the very minimum, it must be shown that she knew of the purpose to which the premises were put. [1970] A.C. 132.

Commentary ....

The decision was confirmed by Misuse of Drugs Act 1971 s.8 which specifically requires proof of knowledge.

> **WARNER V METROPOLITAN POLICE COMMISSIONER 1969**
> The defendant was convicted of possessing amphetamine sulphate, found in a box in his possession which he claimed to believe contained scent.

Held ....

❖ (HL) Defendant's appeal dismissed. "Possession" of drugs is a strict liability offence. It requires proof that the defendant knew he had control over something (which was in fact a drug) but not that he knew that it was a drug. Where the drug is in a container, possession of the container gives rise to an inference of possession of the contents. The defendant may displace this inference by proving that he was mistaken as to the nature (not merely quality) of the contents and, that as a servant or bailee, he had no right to open the container and had no reason to suspect that it contained drugs; or, that as an owner, he received the package innocently and had no reasonable opportunity to ascertain the nature of the contents. [1969] 2 A.C. 256.

Commentary ....

The court stressed that the meaning of "possession" might differ in other contexts. Whilst possessing a drug is strict liability, the case also provides a defence of lack of negligence in "container cases". The offence was re-enacted in the **Misuse of Drugs Act 1971** which specifically provides a no-negligence defence.

Key Principle ....

In determining whether strict liability is a necessary implication, the court may consider whether mens rea words (or defences) appear elsewhere in the statute.

Cundy v Le Cocq 1884

A licensee was charged with selling alcohol to an intoxicated person when neither he nor his servants realised that the purchaser was intoxicated. He was convicted on the basis of strict liability and appealed.

Held

❖ (DC) Appeal dismissed. Other sections of the Licensing Act 1872 use the word "knowingly" whilst s.13, the section under consideration, did not. This was strong evidence that the offence was intended to be one of strict liability. [1884] L.R. 13 Q.B.D. 207.

Commentary

Compare the next case.

Sherras v De Rutzen 1895

The defendant licensee served alcohol to a police constable, believing that he was off-duty.

Held

❖ (DC) Conviction quashed because the offence (contrary to s.16(2) of the **Licensing Act 1872**) required proof of mens rea. Moreover, generally "there is a presumption that mens rea, an evil intention, or knowledge of the wrongfulness of the act, is an essential ingredient in every offence..." per Wright J. [1895] 1 Q.B. 918.

Commentary

The court accepted that the presumption of mens rea may "be displaced ... by the words of the statute creating the offence ..." but was not prepared to infer strict liability simply because the section did not use the word "knowingly" whilst other sections did.

Pharmaceutical Society v Storkwain 1986

The defendants were charged under Medicines Act 1968 s.58(2)(a) with supplying medicine on forged prescriptions. They believed that the prescriptions were valid and were initially acquitted but the Divisional Court held that the offence was strict.

Held

❖ (HL) Defendants' appeal dismissed. Various sections in the Act expressly provided for mens rea and so it could be inferred that the omission to do so in s.58(2)(a) was deliberate. Thus the offence was strict. [1986] 1 W.L.R. 903.

Key Principle

The court may also consider the wording of similar offences in other statutes.

> B (A CHILD) v DIRECTOR OF PUBLIC PROSECUTIONS 2000
> (see p.24). The prosecution argued that s.1(1) of the **Indecency with Children Act 1960** should be read in the light of the Sexual Offences Act 1956. Several sections of the 1956 Act, clearly or by implication, create strict liability in respect of sexual offences involving persons under 16.

Held

❖ (HL) Defendant's appeal allowed. The 1956 Act was a consolidating statute and was "not the product of a rational scheme" per Lord Steyn. It did not display a "clear and coherent pattern" per Lord Nicholls and therefore could not be relied upon to establish strict liability under s.1(1) of the **Indecency With Children Act 1960**. [2000] 2 A.C. 428.

Commentary

Lord Nicholls stated that, generally, the interpretation to be given to a statute could only be gleaned from another statute where that gave "compelling guidance" and consistency of theme. See also the decision in *R. v K* (2001) where liability for indecently assaulting an under aged girl was not strict liability. The provisions of ss.14 and 15 of the **Sexual Offences Act 1956** (now repealed) other than the one under consideration were not conclusive as an aid to interpretation because they were not part of a "single, coherent legislative scheme" per Lord Bingham.

Key Principle

If the words are not conclusive, the presumption of mens rea may be displaced by extrinsic factors such as the subject matter of the offence (including the stigma which it may attract).

> SWEET v PARSLEY 1970
> (see p.29).

Held

❖ (HL) In considering whether an offence is strict, Lord Reid added to *Sherras* that the subject matter of the offence must be taken into account. According to Wright J. in *Sherras*, the offence was one which was "not criminal in any real sense, but ... which (is prohibited) ... in the public interest". According to Lord Reid such "quasi-crimes" are less likely to require mens rea than "truly criminal" acts. When considering the latter, regard must also be given to factors such as the stigma that attaches to the offence, its gravity and whether public interest is served by strict liability. [1970] A.C. 132.

Commentary

In *B (A Child)* (2000), above, Lord Steyn approved the distinction between true and quasi crimes. Section 1(1) of the **Indecency with Children Act 1960** fell within the former category. The seriousness of the offence, the social stigma attached and the broad terms in which it was drawn all militated against strict liability.

> **GAMMON LTD V ATTORNEY-GENERAL OF HONG KONG 1985**
> The defendants were convicted of offences under a Building Ordinance for deviating from plans and carrying out works in a way likely to risk injury or damage.

Held

❖ (PC) Defendants' appeal dismissed. The conditions to be considered in determining whether an offence is strict are:

(1) the presumption of mens rea;

(2) the presumption is strongest where the offence is "truly criminal" in nature;

(3) "the presumption ... can be displaced only if this is clearly or by necessary implication the effect of the statute"; and

(4) "the only situation in which the presumption can be displaced is where the statute is concerned with an issue of social concern, and public safety is such an issue...".

Since the overall purpose of the Ordinance was the protection of public safety, the offences were ones of strict liability. [1985] 1 A.C. 1.

Commentary

(1) In the next case, *Lim Chin Aik* (1963), Lord Evershed also referred to the relevance of the subject matter in deciding on strict liability. He said that such liability was frequently inferred where the subject was the regulation of public welfare.

(2) Other examples where the court has referred to social concern or grave social evil as a reason for imposing strict liability include the supply of medicines: *Storkwain* (1986), pollution: *Alphacell* (1972) and the possession of drugs: *Warner* (1969). In *R. v Prince* (1875) a similar argument was used in the case of abduction. Prior to *B (A Child)* (2000) it had been assumed that *Prince* created a general principle of strict liability in relation to age-based sexual offences. However, this was rejected in *B (A Child)* despite recognition that sexual exploitation of the young was a great social evil. The case confirms that grave social evil is not the only consideration. This point was also made by Lord Evershed in *Lim Chin Aik* (1963).

Key Principle ....

Generally, strict liability should not be imposed unless it will promote greater vigilance and assist in preventing the offence.

> LIM CHIN AIK V R. 1963
> The defendant was convicted of contravening a statutory provision regarding entry to Singapore. An order prohibiting his entry was issued but there was no evidence that he was aware of this.

Held ....

❖ (PC) Defendant's appeal allowed. The offence required proof of mens rea. In addition to considering the social evil, regard must be given to whether strict liability would "assist in the enforcement of the regulations.... Where ... strict liability would result in ... conviction of a class of persons whose conduct could not in any way affect the observance of the law ... even where the statute is dealing with a grave social evil, strict liability is not likely to be intended." [1963] A.C. 160.

> GAMMON LTD V ATTORNEY-GENERAL OF HONG KONG 1985
> (see p.33).

Held ....

❖ (PC) "The presumption of mens rea stands unless it can be shown that the creation of strict liability will be effective to promote the objects of the statute by encouraging greater vigilance to prevent the commission of the offence." Their Lordships concluded that imposing strict liability would help to do so in this case. [1985] 1 A.C. 1.

Commentary ....

In *Storkwain* (1986) (see p.33), Lord Goff rejected the argument that strict liability should not be imposed because it would not "tend towards greater efficiency on the part of pharmacists in detecting forged prescriptions". However, in *Sweet v Parsley* (1970) (see p.29), Lord Reid was influenced by the fact that even "[t]he greatest vigilance cannot prevent tenants ... from smoking cannabis ... in their own rooms" and Lord Diplock stated that "strict liability should not easily be inferred, particularly if there is nothing the defendant could do to improve, influence or control the situation". Moreover, another factor taken into account in rejecting strict liability in *B (A Child)* (2000) was the fact that, according to Lord Nicholls, "there is no general agreement that strict liability is necessary to the enforcement of the law protecting children in sexual matters". Compare this view with that of the legislature as evidenced in the **Sexual Offences Act 2003**. For example in *R. v G* (2008) the House of Lords confirmed that the offence of raping a child under the age of 13, contrary to s.5 of the **Sexual Offences Act 2003**, is strict liability so that mistaken belief that the child is over the age of 13 is not relevant. This meant that the 15-year-old defendant was guilty even though the girl had told him that she was 15 and had consented to the intercourse. In this case, the House also ruled that strict liability offences are not incompatible with the right to a fair trial or the presumption of innocence under article 6 of the European Convention for the Protection of Human Rights and Fundamental Freedoms.

THINK POINT

....

Imagine that it has been discovered that a food additive, called Mixolite, is harmful to human health and Parliament has passed the Mixolite Prohibition Act. This states in section 1 that it is an offence to use, cause or permit Mixolite to be used in the production of any food and in section 2 that "it is an offence to knowingly supply to another person food containing Mixolite". The penalty is a fine of £500. Doreen supplies her chef, Edward, with tins of tomatoes that she does not realise contain Mixolite. Edward does not realise that the tomatoes contain Mixolite either and he uses them in a recipe for lasagne which Doreen then sells in her restaurant. Using the principles contained in this chapter, consider the factors that a court would take into account in deciding whether the offences under the Mixolite Prohibition Act are strict liability and so whether Edward is guilty, under s.1, of using Mixolite in the lasagne and whether Doreen is guilty, under s.1, of causing or permitting Mixolite to be used and, under s.2, of supplying food containing Mixolite.

....

Non-Fatal Offences Against the Person

COMMON ASSAULT AND BATTERY

Key Principle

The actus reus of assault involves an act causing apprehension of unlawful personal violence.

> **FAGAN V METROPOLITAN POLICE COMMISSIONER 1969**
> (see Ch.1, p.1).

Held

❖ (DC) Deciding that assault cannot be committed by omission, the court defined assault as "an act which ... causes another person to apprehend immediate and unlawful personal violence". [1969] 1 Q.B. 439.

Commentary

Apprehension of violence is satisfied by proof of anticipation of a battery. The actus reus includes that the force apprehended be unlawful, according to *Williams* (1984) (confirmed in *Beckford*).

Key Principle

The victim must apprehend immediate force or violence.

> **R. V IRELAND & BURSTOW 1998**
> Ireland was convicted of assault occasioning actual bodily harm, having made repeated silent telephone calls to the victims, causing them psychological damage.

Held

❖ (HL) Appeal dismissed. Silent telephone calls were capable of amounting to assault if the victim apprehended immediate unlawful violence. [1998] A.C. 147.

Commentary

This allows for a liberal interpretation of immediacy. Whether or not there is an assault depends on all the circumstances, including what it was that the victim apprehended. The case also confirms that assault can be committed by words alone. A similar position on both points had been taken in *R. v Constanza* (1997) (CA).

Key Principle

The actus reus of battery involves using unlawful force without the victim's consent.

> FAGAN V METROPOLITAN POLICE COMMISSIONER 1969
> (see Ch.1, p.1).

Held

❖ (DC) Deciding that battery cannot be committed by omission, the court defined battery as the "use of unlawful force to another person without his consent". [1969] 1 Q.B. 439.

Commentary

(1) The term "force" is satisfied simply by proof of contact (or "touching", see *Faulkner v Talbot* (1981)) and the force must be unlawful (see *Williams* (1984)). It has also been suggested, obiter, in *Haystead v Chief Constable of Derbyshire* (2000) that it is probably not necessary to show that the force was directly inflicted.

(2) Exceptionally, in *R. v Santana Bermudez* (2003) a battery was committed by omission where the defendant had falsely informed a police officer who was about to search him that he had no needles. The officer was pricked by a needle in his pocket. Applying *R. v Miller* (1993) (see p.4), the defendant was under a duty to counteract the danger he had created.

Key Principle

Consent to contact generally prevents liability.

> ATTORNEY-GENERAL'S REFERENCE (NO.6 OF 1980)
> Two young men agreed to settle an argument by fighting and one sustained a bleeding nose and bruises. The other was acquitted of

assault on a direction that the agreement to fight (and the use of reasonable force) prevented liability.

Held

❖ (QBD) Consent was no defence for reasons given below but "ordinarily if the victim consents, the assailant is not guilty". [1981] 2 All E.R. 1057.

Commentary

It was also confirmed in *R. v Brown* (1994) (see p.41) that consent may be a defence to assault.

Key Principle

Consent to contact does not necessarily include consent to the consequences of the contact.

> R. v DICA 2004
>
> The defendant was HIV positive and had unprotected consensual sexual intercourse with two women in the course of long-term relationships with them. Both became infected as a result. It was not alleged that the defendant had intended to infect the women. The defendant was convicted of recklessly inflicting grievous bodily harm, contrary to s.20 of the **Offences Against the Person Act 1861.**

Held

❖ (CA) Defendant's appeal allowed, retrial ordered for reasons explained below. Consent to the act of sexual intercourse is not to be regarded "as consent to the risk of consequent disease". [2004] 3 All E.R. 593.

Commentary

This reversed the decision in *R. v Clarence* (1889), where the defendant was held not to have assaulted his wife because she had consented to the act (of sexual intercourse) which had caused her infection with venereal disease. According to *Dica* there are two issues for consideration in these cases: consent to the sexual intercourse and consent to the risk of injury or infection. Consent to the former is not consent to the latter.

Key Principle

Fraud or mistake as to the identity of the actor may vitiate consent.

R. v Richardson (1998)

A disqualified dentist treated patients who would not have consented if they had known she had been suspended from practice . She appealed against her conviction for assault which had been based on vitiation of consent due to her fraud.

Held

❖ (CA) Appeal allowed. The patients were not mistaken as to the nature and quality of the act (dental treatment) nor were they mistaken about the defendant's identity (who she was). [1998] Cr. App. R. 200.

Commentary

One aspect of *Clarence* which was not reversed in *Dica* was the ruling that mistake vitiates consent only if it relates to the nature and quality of the act or to the identity of the defendant. *Richardson* applied that ruling, the Court of Appeal refusing to accept that the defendant's "identity" extended to include her qualifications or attributes. Contrast this decision with the next case.

Key Principle

A mistake as to the nature or quality of the act may, in some circumstances, vitiate consent.

R. v Tabassum 2000

The defendant obtained consent for a breast examination from three women. He had indicated that he was involved in a breast cancer survey and the women consented in the mistaken belief that he had relevant medical qualifications or training. The defendant appealed against conviction for indecent assault.

Held

❖ (CA) Appeal dismissed. The women consented to what they believed was a medical examination by a person with medical qualifications. Although they had consented to the nature of the act (a breast examination) their consent was vitiated because they had not consented to its quality. [2000] 2 Cr.App.R. 328.

Commentary

This is the first case to suggest that mistakes as to the quality of the act (rather than as to its nature) may vitiate consent. It was Tabassum's lack of medical qualifications that affected the quality of the act. This should be compared with *R. v Richardson* (1998) which was argued as a case of mistaken identity rather than as one of mistake as to nature or quality of the act. It may be possible to distinguish *Tabassum* as a case where the lack of qualifications affected the purpose of the act.

Key Principle

Subject to public policy exceptions, consent is no defence where actual bodily harm is caused and was a likely or an intended consequence of the assault.

> R. v DONOVAN 1934
>
> The defendant caused bruising in the course of consensually caning a woman for sexual gratification. He appealed against conviction for indecent and common assault.

Held

❖ (CCA) Appeal allowed. Nevertheless, the court indicated that, generally, consent was no defence where actual bodily harm was intended or a probable consequence of the activity. Public policy exceptions to the rule included "mutual manly contests" and "rough and undisciplined sport or play, where there is no anger and no intention to cause bodily harm". [1934] 2 K.B. 498.

Commentary

For the meaning of actual bodily harm, see below. An example of one of the exceptions noted in *Donovan* is illustrated in *Jones* (1986) where "rough and undisciplined play", causing grievous bodily harm, gave rise to no liability because the defendants did not intend to cause harm and believed that the victim consented. In *Attorney-General's Reference (No.6 of 1980)* (1981), the court held that consent was no defence where actual bodily harm was intended and/or caused because "it is not in the public interest that people should try to cause or should cause each other actual bodily harm for no good reason". It made no difference whether the fight occurred in public or private. The public interest exceptions included properly conducted games and sports, lawful chastisement, reasonable surgical interference and dangerous exhibitions. An example of the position regarding injuries sustained in sporting events can be found in *R. v Barnes* (2005) (CA).

R. v Brown 1994

The defendants caused actual bodily harm and wounding in the course of consensual sado-masochistic activities. They were convicted and appealed.

Held

❖ (HL) Appeals dismissed. Public policy and public interest did not require that the defence of consent be extended to inflicting bodily harm in the course of sado-masochistic practices. [1994] 1 A.C. 212.

Commentary

(1) The policy exceptions mentioned in *Donovan* and *Attorney-General's Reference* (1981) were noted and male ritual circumcision and tattooing were added. The majority rejected the defence argument that the activities in *Brown* were of a sexual nature (in which case consent might have been a defence). In the court's view, sado-masochism was "violent", "cruel" and "degrading" behaviour and so there was no public interest in allowing consent as a defence. This can be contrasted with the decision in *R. v Wilson* (1997). In *Wilson*, the Court of Appeal held that consent was a defence to inflicting actual bodily harm when the defendant burned his initials into his wife's buttocks (at her instigation). The activity lacked the extreme and aggressive element present in *Brown* and was akin to tattooing. Public policy and interest did not demand that such an activity, carried out consensually between spouses in private, should amount to an offence. *Wilson* was distinguished in *R. v Emmett* (1999) where the defendant caused harm to his female sexual partner in the course of consensual sado-masochistic practices. The activities included semi-asphyxiation and the infliction of third-degree burns. *R. v Brown* (1994) was applied because of the nature of the activities and injuries: one was life-threatening and the other involved very serious injury.

(2) Clearly, subject to public policy exceptions such as surgical operations, consent is no defence to the *intentional* infliction of serious bodily harm. For example, it was observed in *Dica* (above), that, applying the principle in *Brown*, consent is no defence to being deliberately infected with HIV. However the case held that one can validly consent to the *risk* of infection during sexual intercourse (i.e. to reckless infliction of HIV) and therefore Dica was entitled to have his defence of consent left to the jury,

(3) The principle has been stated (in both the *Attorney-General's Reference (No.6 of 1980)* and *Brown*) as being that, apart from public policy exceptions, consent is no defence where bodily harm is either intended or caused. This

suggests that consent is no defence where actual bodily harm is caused, even though neither party intended it or even foresaw that it might occur. That is too wide. In *R. v Slingsby* (1995) it was held that the defendant did not commit assault (or constructive manslaughter) having caused the death of his sexual partner by consensually engaging in an activity which neither of them realised would cause serious injury. Thus her consent to the act was a valid consent.

Key Principle

The mens rea of assault and battery is satisfied by either intention or recklessness.

> ### R. v VENNA 1976
> The defendant was convicted of assault occasioning actual bodily harm, having fractured a bone in a policeman's hand whilst being arrested. He appealed against a direction that recklessness was sufficient mens rea for battery.

Held

❖ (CA) Appeal dismissed. The mens rea of battery "is satisfied by proof that the defendant intentionally or recklessly applied force to the person of another". [1976] Q.B. 421.

Commentary

The same mens rea satisfies assault (intentionally or recklessly causing another person to apprehend violence). Moreover, according to *Williams* (see Ch.1), the mens rea extends to the element of "unlawfulness" so that a belief that force is lawful denies the prosecution case. The mens rea similarly extends to "lack of consent", **Offences Against the Person Act 1861** s.47.

Key Principle

Offences Against the Person Act 1861 s.47 requires proof of common assault or battery.

> ### R. v VENNA 1976
> (see above).

Commentary

Both this and *Williams* are cases of assault occasioning actual bodily harm under s.47 where liability turned on proving a common assault (or battery). The common assault/battery must cause the actual bodily harm in fact and law. For the rules on causation, see Ch.1 and, for example, *R. v Roberts* (1971) (see p.42).

Key Principle

"Actual bodily harm" is temporary or permanent bodily injury, not so "trivial as to be wholly insignificant".

> R. v Donovan 1934
> (see p.40).

Held

❖ (CCA) "Bodily harm has its ordinary meaning and includes any hurt or injury calculated to interfere with the health or comfort of the prosecutor ... it need not be permanent but must ... be more than merely transient and trifling". [1934] 2 K.B. 498.

Commentary

In *R. (on the application of T) v DPP* (2003) this was interpreted to include a momentary loss of consciousness which though "transitory" was not "trifling". Also cutting off a substantial amount of someone's hair (without their consent) amounted to causing actual bodily harm in *DPP v Smith* (2006).

Key Principle

Actual bodily harm includes psychiatric injury.

> R. v Ireland & Burstow 1998
> (see pp.36 and 45).

Held

❖ (HL) Recognisable psychiatric illness is capable of amounting to bodily harm. [1998] A.C. 147.

Commentary

This case approves the decision in *R. v Chan Fook* (1994) that psychiatric injury (which is more than "fear, distress or panic") does amount to actual bodily harm. However, the prosecution must produce expert evidence to prove that the defendant has suffered psychiatric injury. In *R. v Dhaliwal* (2006) the Court of Appeal declined to extend the law, holding that psychological symptoms not amounting to psychiatric illness do not constitute actual bodily harm.

Key Principle

The mens rea of s.47 is the same as for common assault and does not require proof of mens rea in relation to the actual bodily harm.

> #### R. v ROBERTS 1971
>
> The defendant was convicted of s.47, after assaulting a woman in his car by trying to remove her coat. She jumped from the car, sustaining actual bodily harm. The defendant's appeal included the claim that it was necessary to prove that he foresaw that she might jump from the car.

Held

❖ (CA) Appeal dismissed. The prosecution must prove that the defendant caused the injury in fact and law. This was established since the woman's response was reasonably foreseeable as likely to happen as a result of the defendant's conduct. It was not necessary to show that he foresaw that this might happen. (1971) 56 Cr.App.R. 95.

Commentary

(1) The chain of causation is broken if the victim does something "so daft" that the reasonable person would not foresee it (see Ch.1).

(2) *Roberts* was approved in *Savage and Parmenter* (1992) where the House of Lords confirmed that the prosecution only have to prove the mens rea of assault and not intention or recklessness vis-a-vis the actual bodily harm.

OFFENCES AGAINST THE PERSON ACT 1861 S.20

Key Principle

The actus reus of s.20 requires proof of either wounding or an infliction of grievous bodily harm. A wound requires proof that the whole continuity of the skin is broken.

C. v EISENHOWER 1984

The defendant shot the victim with an air pistol causing bruising and rupturing internal blood vessels in his eye. The defendant appealed against conviction for s.20 on the basis that there was no wound.

Held

❖ (DC) Appeal allowed. Breaking the skin of an internal cavity is sufficient where that skin is continuous with the outer skin of the body. A ruptured blood vessel in itself was insufficient evidence of a break in the continuity of the whole skin. [1984] 1 Q.B. 331.

Commentary

The epidermis and dermis must be broken for there to be a wound.

Key Principle

Grievous bodily harm means "serious bodily harm".

DPP v SMITH 1961

The defendant caused the death of a policeman, who was hanging onto his car, by driving the car into oncoming traffic.

Held

❖ (HL) In dealing with murder, the House commented that grievous bodily harm bears "its ordinary and natural meaning". The meaning of "bodily harm" was self-evident and grievous meant "really serious". [1961] A.C. 290

Commentary

Grievous bodily harm includes serious psychiatric injury (*R. v Ireland & Burstow* (1998) (see below)).

Key Principle

"Inflicting" can occur without physical violence being applied directly or indirectly to the victim.

R. v IRELAND & BURSTOW 1998

Burstow, a "stalker", had harassed the victim in a number of ways causing her severe depression. He appealed against conviction on the basis that he could not be said to have inflicted grievous bodily harm because he had not come into contact with the victim.

Held ....

❖ (HL) Appeal dismissed. Direct or indirect application of force was not a necessary element of the offence. [1998] A.C. 147.

Commentary ....

The House of Lords rejected the argument that assault or battery were necessary elements of the offence. This was applied in *R. v Dica* (2004) which expressly overruled *R. v Clarence* (1889) on this point.

Key Principle ....

The mens rea of s.20 requires proof that the defendant intended or foresaw the risk of some physical harm.

R. v SAVAGE AND PARMENTER 1992

Savage intended to throw the contents of a glass at the victim but let go of the glass, causing a wound. She was convicted under s.20 but because of a misdirection on the mens rea of s.20 of the offence, the Court of Appeal substituted a verdict of s.47. Parmenter was convicted of causing grievous bodily harm to his baby. The Court of Appeal quashed his conviction and declined to substitute a verdict of guilty under s.47. Both cases raised the same issues on appeal.

Held ....

❖ (HL) Appeal by the defendant in *Savage* dismissed. Prosecution's appeal in *Parmenter* allowed and conviction under s.47 substituted.

(1) Section 47 could be established even though the defendant did not intend actual bodily harm and was not reckless as to causing it. Therefore both defendants could be convicted under s.47 (and the Court of Appeal had reached the wrong conclusion in the case of *Parmenter*).

(2) It was not necessary, under s.20, to prove that the defendant intended or foresaw a wound or serious physical injury. Intention or recklessness as to some physical harm, albeit minor, was sufficient. [1992] 1 A.C. 699.

Commentary ....

These cases also establish that a verdict of s.47 can be returned on a charge of s.20.

OFFENCES AGAINST THE PERSON ACT 1861, S.18

Key Principle

Section 18, like s.20, requires proof of a wound or grievous bodily harm but, unlike s.20, refers to causing rather than inflicting grievous bodily harm. The word "cause" is wider than the word "inflict".

> R. v MANDAIR 1995
>
> The defendant caused serious injury to his wife. He was charged under s.18 with causing grievous bodily harm with intent and found guilty of causing grievous bodily harm contrary to s.20 on a direction that this was an alternative, lesser verdict open to the jury.

Held

❖ (HL) "Causing grievous bodily harm" (s.18) could occur by inflicting the harm or by causing it in some other way. Since the word "cause" was wide enough to cover "infliction", a verdict under s.20 was possible on a charge under s.18. Although the verdict of "causing grievous bodily harm contrary to s.20" was inappropriate because the offence under s.20 is one of "inflicting grievous bodily harm", there had been no miscarriage of justice. [1995] 1 A.C. 208.

Commentary

(1) Whilst this case suggests a difference between "causing" and "inflicting" grievous bodily harm, in *Ireland & Burstow,* Lord Hope suggested that, for all practical purposes, there is no difference between "cause" and "inflict" beyond the latter implying something detrimental to the victim.

(2) Section 18 is a crime of specific intent requiring proof of an intention to cause grievous bodily harm or to resist or prevent arrest. Intent means the same as in murder, foresight of virtual certainty being evidence of intent: *R. v Bryson* (1985). It is as yet undecided but seems virtually certain that *Woollin* (1998) (see Ch.2) applies to intent under this section.

> **THINK POINT**
>
> Read *R. v Dica* [2004] 3 All E.R. 593 carefully and then consider the following questions:

The defendant in *R. v Dica* was charged, contrary to s.20 **Offences Against the Person Act 1861**, with inflicting grievous bodily harm on his victims. Did the court feel that he could have been found guilty of rape if he had been charged with the offence? You will also find the answer by looking at *R. v B* (2006) (see p.51).

In *R. v Dica*, Judge L.J. stated that 'the position here is analogous to that considered in *R v Tabassum* (2000)'. Does the decision in *R. v Dica* support the decision reached in *R. v Tabassum* or does it contradict it?

Is there anything in the judgment that suggests that the principle in *R. v Dica* (that consent can be a defence) is restricted to cases of recklessly infecting a sexual partner with an STD or that might it apply to the reckless infliction of grievous bodily harm more generally?

Sexual Offences

....

5

RAPE: THE ACTUS REUS

Key Principle ....

The actus reus of rape requires proof of non-consensual penile penetration of vagina, anus or mouth. (**Sexual Offences Act 2003** s.1(1)).

Commentary ....

(1) The actus reus of rape was originally restricted to vaginal penetration. This definition was extended by the Criminal Justice and Public Order Act 1994 to include anal penetration. Section 1(1) of the **Sexual Offences Act 2003** represents a further extension of the definition and includes oral penetration.

(2) The term "sexual intercourse" has been replaced by the term "penetration" but the crime is still gender specific in that it requires that the penetration be by penis. However this, like all references to body parts in the Act, now specifically includes those that have been surgically reconstructed: s.79(3). Section 79(2) of the Act preserves the effect of *Kaitamaki v R.* (1985) by providing that "penetration is a continuing act from entry to withdrawal".

(3) In all cases where the complainant is aged 13 or above, the prosecution must establish that the penetration was non-consensual in order to prove rape. The meaning of consent is explored in the next key principles. Where the complainant is aged under 13, rape occurs irrespective of consent: s.5 of the **Sexual Offences Act 2003**. Where the complainant is aged between 13 and 16 (or 18 in the case of abuse of trust), there is an alternative charge to rape for cases of consensual penetration. This is the offence of sexual activity with a child contrary to s.9 (and s.16 in the case of abuse of trust).

Key Principle ....

A person does not consent to penetration if the defendant intentionally deceived that person as to the nature or purpose of the act. (**Sexual Offences Act 2003** s.76(2)(a)).

Commentary

(1) This preserves the decision in cases such as *R. v Flattery* (1877) where the defendant was convicted of rape, having intentionally deceived the complainant into believing that the act of sexual intercourse was a surgical operation. For a further example, see the case of *R. v Williams* (1923).

(2) It is less clear what the effect of the Act might be on other previous decisions because it is not yet clear how the court will interpret the meaning of the words "nature" and "purpose" in the Act. It is possible that the word "nature" might be interpreted narrowly in line with the decision in the now otherwise discredited authority of *R. v Clarence* (1889) (see Ch.4, p.38). An alternative approach might be that adopted in *R. v Tabassum* (2000) (see Ch.4 p.39) although this suggests that a mistake as to the quality of the act (rather than its nature) might also vitiate consent. Deliberate deception as to the purpose of the act (s.76(2)(a)) would cover where a defendant deliberately deceives the complainant about why the act is being done. This is illustrated in the case of *R. v Devonald* (2008) which involved the issue of consent in the crime of causing another to engage in a sexual activity without consent contrary to s.4 of the **Sexual Offences Act 2003**. The defendant corresponded with the victim through the Internet and, posing as a 20-year-old woman, persuaded him to masturbate in front of a webcam. The victim believed that he was doing so for the sexual gratification of the woman that the defendant pretended to be and so had been deceived as to the purpose of the act.

(3) For rape, s.76(2)(a) only applies if the deceit is about the nature or purpose of the act of intercourse. Other forms of deceit are dealt with under s.74, see, for example, *R. v Jheeta* (2007) at p.51.

Key Principle

A person does not consent to penetration if the defendant intentionally induced the consent by impersonating a person known personally to the complainant. (**Sexual Offences Act 2003** s.76(2)(b)).

Commentary

This provision confirms and possibly extends the law beyond the decision in *R. v Elbekkay* (1995) where a woman had consented to penetration in the belief that the defendant was her co-habitee. The defendant appealed against conviction on the basis that whilst rape included intercourse obtained by impersonation of a husband (**Sexual Offences Act 1956** s.1(2)), the same did not apply to other cases of impersonation. The Court of Appeal dismissed the appeal and held that the question was simply whether the woman consented (*Olugboja* (1982)) and she had not consented to intercourse with the defendant in this case.

Key Principle

In all other cases, a person consents to penetration if s/he agrees by choice and has the freedom and capacity to make that choice. (**Sexual Offences Act 2003** s.74).

R. v JHEETA 2007

The defendant's girlfriend was deceived into having intercourse with the defendant by him posing as a police officer and sending her false text messages. The messages asserted that the defendant was suicidal and instructed the girlfriend, who wanted to break up with the defendant, to have intercourse with him, suggesting that otherwise she would be fined. She would not have had intercourse with the defendant were it not for the messages. The defendant pleaded guilty to rape on the basis that the situation fell within s.76(2)(a) of the **Sexual Offences Act 2003**. He appealed against sentence and the Court of Appeal gave leave to appeal against conviction.

Held

❖ (CA) Appeal dismissed. The complainant had been deceived about the situation in which she found herself rather than being deceived as to the nature or purpose of the act of intercourse. Therefore the conclusive presumption of lack of consent under s.76(2)(a) did not apply. However the deception meant that she had not consented by "free choice" under s.74. [2007] EWCA Crim 1699.

Commentary

(1) Section 74 provides statutory guidance where previously the matter was left to the decision of the jury: see *R. v Olugboja* (1982).

(2) One might expect that the facts of a case like *R. v Clarence* would, as in *Jheeta*, be caught by this section. However, in *R. v B* (2006) the Court of Appeal held that the validity of consent to intercourse (through freedom and capacity to choose) is not affected by the defendant failing to disclose that he is HIV positive.

(3) According to *R. v Bree* (2007) where the complainant is voluntarily intoxicated at the time of the intercourse, it is necessary to distinguish between cases where consent occurs despite the intoxication and cases where the complainant has lost the capacity to choose whether to consent or not.

Key Principle ....

There is a presumption that consent is lacking in certain situations. The presumption may be rebutted by evidence from the defendant. (**Sexual Offences Act 2003** s.75(1)).

Key Principle ....

The circumstances in which there is a rebuttable presumption of lack of consent are:

Section 75(2)(a): where "any person was, at the time of the relevant act or immediately before it began, using violence against the complainant or causing the complainant to fear that immediate violence would be used against him".

Section 75(2)(b): where "any person was, at the time of the relevant act or immediately before it began, causing the complainant to fear that violence was being used or that immediate violence would be used against any person".

Section 75(2)(c): where "the complainant was, and the defendant was not, unlawfully detained" at the relevant time.

Section 75(2)(d): where "the complainant was asleep or otherwise unconscious" at the relevant time.

Section 75(2)(e): where "because of the complainant's physical disability, the complainant would not have been able to communicate to the defendant whether the complainant consented" at the relevant time.

Section 75(2)(f): where "any person had administered to or caused to be taken by the complainant, without the complainant's consent, a substance which, having regard to when it was administered or taken, was capable of causing or enabling the complainant to be stupefied or overpowered" at the relevant time.

RAPE: THE FAULT ELEMENT

Key Principle
The fault element of rape is satisfied by proof that the defendant intentionally penetrates without reasonable belief that the complainant is consenting. (**Sexual Offences Act 2003** s.1(1)).

Commentary
(1) Section 1(2) provides that all the circumstances should be taken into account in deciding whether the defendant's belief in consent was reasonable or not. This includes the steps that he took to ascertain whether there was consent.

(2) Rape has now become a crime of negligence rather than intention or recklessness. This dispenses with the rule laid down in *DPP v Morgan* (1976) (see Ch.2). Whilst it is still the case that an honest mistaken belief is inconsistent with mens rea it is no longer the case that liability for rape is restricted to situations where the defendant had mens rea. By turning the crime into one of negligence, mistake about consent will still excuse a defendant but only if it is based on reasonable grounds.

(3) Section 76 (above) also provides that the defendant cannot claim that he reasonably believed that the complainant consented where the conditions for subss.(a) and (b) are met. Section 75 (above) provides for an evidential burden on the defendant to rebut the presumption that he did not reasonably believe that the complainant consented where the conditions in subss.(a)-(f) apply.

ASSAULT BY PENETRATION: THE ACTUS REUS

Key Principle
The actus reus is committed by the non-consensual sexual penetration of vagina or anus of another person. (**Sexual Offences Act 2003** s.2(1)).

Commentary
(1) This creates a new offence to cover those cases of sexual penetration that only amounted to indecent assault under the old law. The offence covers sexual penetration with "a part of his body or anything else" and so can be committed by either sex. As for rape, penetration remains a continuing act.

(2) The meaning of non-consensual is the same as for rape (see above). Where the complainant is aged under 13, liability arises irrespective of

consent: s.6. In the case of complainants aged between 13 and 16 (or 18 in the cases of abuse of trust) lack of consent must be proven in order to establish assault by penetration. However consensual acts of penetration may give rise to the alternative charge of sexual activity with a child (contrary to s.9 or s.16 in cases of abuse of trust).

(3) The penetration must be sexual and guidance on the meaning of this term is provided in s.78 (see below under sexual assault).

ASSAULT BY PENETRATION: THE FAULT ELEMENT

Key Principle

The fault element is satisfied by proof that the defendant intentionally penetrates without reasonable belief that the complainant is consenting. (**Sexual Offences Act 2003** s.2(1)).

Commentary

Section 2(2) provides that all the circumstances should be taken into account in deciding whether the defendant's belief in consent was reasonable or not. This includes the steps that he took to ascertain whether there was consent. Like rape this is a crime of negligence so that a mistaken belief in consent will only exonerate if it is based on reasonable grounds. Sections 75 and 76 (see above) also apply to this offence.

SEXUAL ASSAULT: THE ACTUS REUS

Key Principle

The actus reus involves a sexual touching without the consent of the person being touched. (**Sexual Offences Act 2003** s.3).

Commentary

(1) Touching is defined in s.79(8) as touching "with any part of the body, with anything else [and] through anything". It is confirmed in *R. v H* (2005) see p.55 that touching a person includes touching their clothes. The Act replaces the previous offence of indecent assault although it appears to be more limited in scope. Under the old law, indecent assault could be committed by assault or battery: *Fairclough v Whipp* (1951). Section 3 can be committed by touching (battery) only. The definition of touching is not wide enough to cover cases where the defendant does not come into contact with the complainant but does cause her or him to believe that s/he will. In some cases this

conduct might be caught by alternative offence found in ss.4 and 62 as confirmed in *R. v H* (2005) below.

(2) The meaning of non-consensual is subject to the same principles as in rape and the above discussion about the continued applicability of cases such as *R. v Tabassum* (2000) apply equally here. The case law relating to consent, examined in Ch.4, may also be a relevant consideration in cases of sexual assault.

(3) The touching must be sexual and guidance on the meaning of this term is provided in s.78 (below).

Key Principle
Touching is sexual if a reasonable person would consider it, because of its nature, sexual. (**Sexual Offences Act 2003** s.78(a)).

Commentary
Subsection (a) further provides that in these cases it does not matter what the defendant's purpose is. This is similar to the test under the old law of indecent assault. See *R. v Court* (1989) (below) where Lord Ackner indicated that motive was irrelevant in cases of inherently (unambiguously) indecent assaults. The prosecution did not have to prove an indecent purpose in order to secure a conviction.

Key Principle
Touching is sexual if its nature is ambiguous but it is rendered sexual by the circumstances and/or the purpose of any person in relation to it. (**Sexual Offences Act 2003** s.78(b)).

> **R. v H 2005**
> The defendant approached the victim, saying 'Do you fancy a shag' and grabbed her tracksuit bottoms attempting to pull her towards him. The defendant was convicted of sexual assault and appealed.

Held
❖ (CA) Appeal dismissed. The touching was not inevitably sexual under s.78(a). It did however satisfy the two requirements under s.78(b). The first being that the touching itself, ignoring the circumstances, might be sexual and the second that it was sexual as indicated by the circumstances, including what the defendant had said. [2005] EWCA Crim 732.

Commentary

(1) This is also similar to the test used in *R. v Court* (1989) to determine the presence of "indecency" in indecent assault. Court had spanked a girl several times across her clothed buttocks. He admitted that the reason for doing so had been a "buttocks fetish". In cases where the assault was not inherently indecent but was objectively capable of being regarded as indecent, the House of Lords held that evidence concerning the defendant's motive or intention could be introduced to determine whether the act was indecent or not. Indecent intention was therefore a necessary element in some cases of "ambiguous indecency".

(2) The Act does not provide a definition of "sexual". The definition of "indecent" prior to the Act is clearly not applicable. This had been explained in *R. v Court* (1989) as where "right-minded persons would consider the conduct ... so offensive to contemporary standards of modesty and privacy as to be indecent". "Sexual" appears to be a broader term than "indecent" and its meaning will need clarification.

SEXUAL ASSAULT: THE MENS REA

Key Principle

The fault element is satisfied by proof that the defendant intentionally touched without reasonable belief that the complainant is consenting. (**Sexual Offences Act 2003** s.3(1)).

Commentary

(1) In requiring that the touching be intentional, the Act preserves the previous law governing indecent assault: reckless assault was not sufficient, intention was required: *R. v Parsons* (1993). Nevertheless it is not, apparently, a crime of specific intent: *R v Heard* (2007) (see p.145).

(2) Section 3(2) provides that all the circumstances should be taken into account in deciding whether the defendant's belief in consent was reasonable or not. This includes the steps that he took to ascertain whether there was consent. This is another of the sexual offences that is satisfied by proof of negligence. This dispenses with the decision in *R. v Kimber* (1983) that honest but unreasonable mistaken belief in consent disproves the fault element. Any mistaken belief must now be based on reasonable grounds. Sections 75 and 76 also apply to this offence.

In *R. v Gareth Linekar* [1995] Q.B. 250, the accepted facts were that a prostitute consented to sexual intercourse with the defendant in the belief that she was going to be paid. The defendant did not pay and never had any intention of doing so. He was charged with rape on the basis that his deception vitiated the woman's consent to the intercourse. The Court of Appeal held that consent had not been vitiated because the woman knew the nature of the act and identity of the actor. Do you think that the decision might be different today in the light of s.76(2)(a) or s.74 of the **Sexual Offences Act 2003**?

In *R. v George* [1956] Crim L.R. 52, the defendant was found not guilty of indecent assault (under the old law). His act of removing a girl's shoe was not inherently (in its nature) indecent. Since it was also held not to be objectively capable of being regarded as indecent, the defendant's undisclosed indecent intention (a shoe fetish) could not render the assault indecent. Do you think that the conduct in *George* might now be considered sexual under s.78 and thus a sexual assault contrary to s.3 of the **Sexual Offences Act 2003**? For assistance with the answer consider Lord Woolf's judgment in *R. v H* (2005) (see p.55).

Homicide

. . . .

6

ACTUS REUS

Key Principle
The defendant must cause the death of a human being under the Queen's peace.

> **ATTORNEY-GENERAL'S REFERENCE (NO.3 OF 1994) 1998**
> With intent to cause her grievous bodily harm, the defendant stabbed a pregnant woman in the abdomen. The child was born prematurely because of the stabbing and died as a result of having been premature.

Held
❖ (HL) Homicide can be charged for causing the death of a child, born alive, by injury inflicted (on the foetus or its mother) prior to its birth. [1998] A.C. 245.

Commentary
(1) The position differs if the child is miscarried or stillborn because a foetus cannot be the object of homicide. Based on the hypothesis that the defendant did not intend to harm the foetus (or the child that it would become), the House of Lords rejected liability for murder, refusing to apply the doctrine of transferred malice (see p.23). The situation did however give rise to manslaughter (without the necessity of transferred malice), based on the unlawful act of stabbing the mother.

(2) For the principles relating to factual and legal causation, see Ch.1.

(3) The old principle that death must occur within a year and a day of any injury has been abolished by the Law Reform (Year and a Day Rule) Act 1996. However, the consent of the Attorney-General is required where more than three years have elapsed between the death and the injury (or where the defendant has already been convicted of an offence in respect of the activity).

MURDER: MENS REA

Key Principle

Murder requires proof of intention to kill or intention to cause grievous bodily harm.

> R. v MOLONEY 1985
> (see Ch.2, p.18).

Held

❖ (HL) Malice aforethought (the mens rea of murder) is only established by proof of intention to kill or cause grievous bodily harm. Recklessness is not sufficient. [1985] A.C. 905.

Key Principle

Intention to kill or cause grievous bodily harm can be established if the defendant foresaw death or grievous bodily harm as a virtually certain consequence.

> R. v WOOLLIN 1998
> (see Ch.2, p.19).

Commentary

See also *R. v Moloney* (1985), *R. v Hancock & Shankland* (1986), and *Matthews & Alleyne* (2003) discussed in Ch.2.

VOLUNTARY MANSLAUGHTER: DIMINISHED RESPONSIBILITY

Key Principle

The defendant must prove that s/he was suffering from an abnormality of mental functioning (Coroners and Justice Act 2009 s.52(1))

Commentary

Section 52 of the **Coroners and Justice Act 2009** amends the definition of diminished responsibility laid down in section 2 of the Homicide Act 1957. What used to be called an "abnormality of mind" becomes an "abnormality of mental functioning".

Key Principle ....

The abnormality must arise from a recognised medical condition (**Coroners and Justice Act 2009** s.52(1)(a))

Commentary ....

(1) This is narrower than the old law where the abnormality had to arise from "arrested or retarded development of mind or any inherent causes or induced by disease or injury": **Homicide Act 1957** s.2. Presumably however, a number of conditions that gave rise to the defence would continue to do so, such as psychopathy as in *R. v Byrne* (1960), schizophrenia and schizo-affective disorder as in *R. v Khan (Dawood)* (2009) and depression as in *R. v Alhuwalia* (1992) and *R. v Ramchurch* (2010).

(2) The issues raised under the old law by defendants who killed whilst suffering from alcohol dependency syndrome seem likely to remain under the new law. Clearly, alcohol dependency syndrome is a disease and disorder of the mind: *R. v Stewart* (2009) but that does not necessarily mean that it is also an abnormality of mental functioning. According to *R. v Wood* (2008) the syndrome can be an abnormality, even where brain damage is not caused, as long as it is a severe case. According to *R. v Stewart*, if the syndrome causes the consumption of alcohol to be involuntary and the result of an irresistible craving, this may also be taken into account as an abnormality whilst voluntary intoxication cannot. However the fact that some of the drinking may be voluntary does not deprive the defendant of the defence.

Key Principle ....

The abnormality must substantially impair the defendant's ability to (a) understand the nature of his/her actions and/or (b) form rational judgement and/or (c) exercise self-control (**Coroners and Justice Act 2009** s.52(1)(b), 1(A))

Commentary ....

(1) The effect of the impairment on the defendant's ability is the same as under the old law as laid down in *R. v Byrne* (1960).

(2) Under the old law, "substantial impairment" was taken to mean a more than trivial impairment but not necessarily total impairment: see, for example, *R. v Ramchurch* (2010) where the medical experts disagreed about whether the defendant's depressive disorder gave rise to a substantial impairment. This case, and *R. v Khan (Dawood)* (2009), confirm that whether

or not there has been a substantial impairment is a question for the jury. This probably remains unaffected by the Act.

Key Principle
The abnormality must provide an explanation for the defendant's conduct. (**Coroners and Justice Act 2009** s.52(1)(c))

Commentary
Under the old law, the abnormality did not have to be the sole cause of the defendant's conduct: *R. v Ramchurch* (2010). The new Act specifies (in s.1B) that the abnormality provides an explanation for the conduct if it causes or is a significant contributory factor in causing the conduct but it does not have to be causative.

VOLUNTARY MANSLAUGHTER: LOSS OF CONTROL

Key Principle
The defendant's conduct must result from a loss of self-control. (**Coroners and Justice Act 2009** s.54(1)(c)).

Commentary
(1) The **Coroners and Justice Act 2009** abolishes the old mitigating defence of provocation and replaces it with the defence of loss of self-control. Under the old law there had to be a "sudden and temporary loss of self-control": *R. v Thornton* (1992) which prevented the defence from being available in a number of cases involving women who killed their abusive partners. A time lapse between acts of domestic abuse and the killing and the slow-burn reaction often proved fatal to the defence: *R. v Thornton* (1992), *R. v Ahluwalia* (1992). In s.54(2) the Act specifically removes the requirement that the loss of control be sudden in order to address this and other issues. However it also specifically provides that the defence is not available if the defendant "acted in a considered desire for revenge" (s.54(4)).

(2) It seems likely that factors that were relevant under the old law in determining whether or not there had been a loss of control will remain relevant. These included time lapses as above, "cumulative provocation": *R. v Humphreys* (1995), characteristics of the defendant that impacted on the ability for self-control, such as battered spousal syndrome: *R. v Thornton*

(1996), and self-induced addiction: *R. v Morhall* (1996)) and, subject to the next key principle, the effect of acts aimed at others: *R. v Pearson* (1992).

Key Principle

The loss of self-control must be attributable to either the defendant's fear of serious violence from the victim or to things done or said (or both) which constituted circumstances of an extremely grave character and caused the defendant to have a justifiable sense of being seriously wronged. (**Coroners and Justice Act 2009** s.55)

Commentary

(1) These "qualifying triggers" are to be disregarded if they were caused by the defendant inciting them in order to provide an excuse to use violence: s.55(6).

(2) The first qualifying trigger (fear of serious violence) must be aimed at the defendant or another identified person and would apply in the future to cases such as *R. v Thornton* (1992) and *R. v Alhuwalia* (1992) where the defendants killed abusive partners from whom they feared repeated serious violence.

(3) The conditions for second qualifying trigger (extremely grave circumstances and a justifiable sense of being wronged) are more restrictive than under the previous law and will exclude defendants such as Doughty from the scope of the defence. In *R. v Doughty* (1986) a father killed his 17-day-old baby because he lost his temper due the baby's persistent crying. In s.55(6), the Act also specifically excludes sexual infidelity from being within this qualifying trigger.

Key Principle

The jury must decide whether a person of the defendant's sex and age, with a normal degree of tolerance and self restraint and in the circumstances of the defendant, might have reacted in the same or a similar way. (**Coroners and Justice Act 2009** s.54(1)(c))

Commentary

This puts into statutory form the partly objective, partly subjective test originally discussed in *DPP v Camplin* (1978) where it was decided that the 15-year-old defendant's reaction should be tested against that of a reasonable 15-year-old. In that case Lord Diplock ruled that "the reasonable man ... is a person having the same power of self-control to be expected of an ordinary person of the sex and age of the accused, but in other respects sharing such of the accused characteristics as they think would affect the gravity of the provocation to him...". It also confirms the position adopted in *Attorney-General for Jersey v Holley* (2005) that the standard of self-control to be expected is purely objective ("a normal degree of tolerance and self restraint") and that "the circumstances of the defendant" is a reference to "all of the defendant's circumstances other than those whose only relevance ... is that they bear on the defendant's general capacity for tolerance and self-restraint.": s.54(3).

INVOLUNTARY MANSLAUGHTER: CONSTRUCTIVE LIABILITY

Key Principle
The defendant must commit the actus reus and have any mens rea required for the unlawful act which causes the death.

> R. v LAMB 1967
> The defendant was convicted of manslaughter, having shot and killed a friend. Misunderstanding how the gun worked, neither the defendant nor the victim anticipated injury.

Held
❖ (CA) Defendant's appeal allowed due to a misdirection. There was no unlawful act (assault) without proof of the actus reus and mens rea. Since the latter was missing, the offence was incomplete. [1967] 2 Q.B. 981.

Commentary
There was no actus reus of psychic assault because the victim did not apprehend contact, nor was there physical assault because of lack of mens rea. For further examples, see *Slingsby* (see Ch.4, p.42) where there was no assault because of consent and *R. v Scarlett* (1993) (see Ch.14, p.170) where there was no assault because the force was used in defence of property.

Key Principle
The unlawful act must be established as the cause of the death.

R. v KENNEDY 2007

The defendant prepared a syringe of heroin and presented it ready for use to the deceased, who, acting freely and voluntarily, used it to inject himself and died as a result. The defendant appealed against his conviction for manslaughter.

Held

❖ (HL) Defendant's conviction quashed. The defendant's unlawful act of supplying the loaded syringe did not cause the death because the deceased's act of self-injection broke the chain of causation (see above in Ch.1). Moreover, it was not a dangerous act and thus could not be the basis for a constructive manslaughter conviction (see *Church*, below). The deceased's act of self-injection was not unlawful and the defendant being a party to that lawful act could not be the basis for a constructive manslaughter conviction (following *R. v Dias* (2002)). [2007] 3 W.L.R. 612.

Commentary

(1) If D injects V with the heroin (even with V's consent), that is an unlawful act (administering a noxious substance, contrary to the **Offences Against the Person Act 1861** s.23). It is also dangerous. If it causes V's death, then D will be guilty of constructive manslaughter: *Cato* (1976). If, on the other hand, V injects himself, then, as the present case demonstrates, D will not be guilty of manslaughter—though of course D could be liable for the lesser offence of supplying a controlled drug. The case approves the decision in *R. v Dias* (2002), which had similar facts and overrules the decision in *R. v Rogers* (2003) where the defendant assisted the victim in self-injecting by holding a tourniquet on the victim's arm whilst the victim injected himself. Since the act of self-injecting was lawful, all Rogers had done was assist in a lawful act and so it was held that he was not guilty of manslaughter.

(2) Another example of a case where there was an unlawful act but it did not cause the death is *R. v Dhaliwal* (2006), see Ch.4, where there was an unlawful act of assault but death was caused instead by psychological damage (which was not an unlawful act) caused by a history of abuse.

Key Principle

The unlawful act must also be dangerous, in the sense that the reasonable person would realise that it creates a risk of some physical harm, albeit slight.

R. v CHURCH 1966
(see Ch.1, p.14).

Held

❖ (CA) Defendant's appeal dismissed. In the context of constructive man-slaughter, the "unlawful act must be such as all sober and reasonable people would inevitably recognise must subject the other person to, at least, the risk of some harm ... albeit not serious harm." [1966] 1 Q.B. 59.

Commentary

Attorney-General's Reference (No.3 of 1994) (1998) (see p.58) makes it clear that the "other person" foreseen as subjected to the risk of harm need not be the ultimate victim. In *Dawson* (1985) the defendant and others committed robbery at a garage, using a replica gun. The 60-year-old attendant, who had a severe heart condition, died shortly afterwards from a heart attack. The Court of Appeal quashed the defendant's manslaughter conviction, holding that in determining whether a reasonable person would have recognised the risk of some physical harm (not mere emotional stress), the reasonable person is to be assumed to have had only the knowledge which was available to the defendant (which did not include knowledge of the attendant's heart condition). For a similar decision where the victim was an apparently healthy 15-year-old, see *R. v Carey* (2006). The knowledge imputed to the reasonable man would obviously be more if the frailty and old age of the victim had been obvious to anyone: *Watson* (1989).

Key Principle

The defendant must intend to do the unlawful act but it is not necessary to show that s/he intended or foresaw any harm.

DPP v NEWBURY & JONES 1977

The defendants caused the death of a train guard by pushing a paving stone from a parapet onto a train. They were convicted of manslaughter on a direction that it was not necessary to show that they foresaw harm to a person.

Held

❖ (HL) Defendants' appeal dismissed. Constructive manslaughter requires that the defendant intentionally did the act which is unlawful and dangerous. It is not necessary to prove that s/he knew that it was unlawful or dangerous.

Moreover, following *Church*, the test for "dangerous act" is objective. [1977] A.C. 500.

Commentary

A statement in *R. v Dalby* (1982) that the unlawful act "must be directed at the victim and likely to cause immediate injury, however slight", was later corrected in *R. v Goodfellow* (1986). In *Goodfellow* the defendant had set fire to his council house in order, as he claimed, to persuade the council to re-house him and his family. His wife was killed in the fire. The Court of Appeal, held that he had been properly convicted of manslaughter and that the unlawful act (here arson) did not have to be aimed at any anyone.

INVOLUNTARY MANSLAUGHTER: RECKLESSNESS AND GROSS NEGLIGENCE

Key Principle

Where liability is not based on an unlawful act, the prosecution must prove gross negligence (or, possibly, recklessness).

> **R. v ADOMAKO 1995**
> An anaesthetist failed to notice that a tube supplying oxygen to a patient had become disconnected during an operation. The patient died as a result. The anaesthetist was convicted of manslaughter and appealed.

Held

❖ (HL) In such cases, it is necessary to prove that the breach of a duty of care caused the death and that, in all the circumstances, the breach was so grossly negligent as to be characterised as criminal. [1995] 1 A.C. 171.

Commentary

(1) In *R. v Evans* (2009) the victim's half sister was found guilty of gross negligence manslaughter when she failed to get help for the victim who died as a result of using heroin supplied by the defendant. Despite some previous uncertainty in the law, this case confirms that the question of whether or not a duty of care arises is an issue of law for the judge to decide.

(2) In *R. v Wacker* (2003) the defendant was guilty of gross negligence manslaughter of a number of Chinese people who died in his lorry in which he had attempted to smuggle them into the UK and the ventilator of which he had sealed in order to avoid their detection. It was not open to him to argue that, because he and the victims were engaged in an illegal joint venture, he did not owe the victims a duty of care.

(3) In order to amount to gross negligence, the court required that there be a risk of death run by the defendant. In *R. v Singh (Gurphal)* (1999) the defendant, who helped his father run a lodging house, was found guilty of manslaughter when a lodger died from carbon monoxide poisoning. He was guilty because he was aware of the danger posed by a defective gas fire in the house but had failed to take reasonable care to deal with it. The Court of Appeal confirmed that gross negligence involves proof that "a reasonably prudent person would have foreseen a serious and obvious risk ... of death" per Schiemann J.

(4) In *R. v Misra and Srivastava* (2004) the Court of Appeal held that the definition of manslaughter by gross negligence in *Adomako* did not involve any uncertainty and thus did not infringe art.7 of the European Convention on Human Rights. The question for the jury was not whether the defendant's negligence was gross and whether, additionally, it was a crime, but whether his behaviour was grossly negligent and consequently a crime. It was also held that the breach of duty must expose the victim to the risk, not merely of serious injury, but of death.

(5) The test for gross negligence is entirely objective and does not depend upon proof of subjective recklessness (though proof of subjective recklessness might be relevant in deciding upon the grossness of the conduct): *Attorney-General's Reference (No.2 of 1999)* (2000) (CA). There may, however, be a category of manslaughter by recklessness, which is a separate basis of liability from gross negligence. For a conviction on this basis the prosecution would have to show both (a) that the defendant's actions posed an obvious risk of serious harm and (b) that the defendant had a subjective awareness that his actions involved a high probability of a risk of death or of serious injury: *R. v Lidar* (2000).

THINK POINT

Why do you think that Parliament decided to exclude sexual infidelity from the defence of loss of control?

Can a defendant's mental characteristics, such as brain damage, that make it more difficult for the defendant to exercise self-control be relevant to the test for the defence under s.54 of the **Coroners and Justice Act 2009**?

Do you think that the new definition of diminished responsibility and the new defence of loss of control are narrower or wider than the defences under the previous law. Can you explain your answer?

Consider the following facts. The defendant persuades the victim to help him burn down his business premises so that the defendant can make an insurance claim. The victim is killed in an explosion whilst he and the defendant are setting fire to the building. On what basis might the defendant be guilty of manslaughter? You could check your answer by reading the case of *R. v Willoughby* [2004] EWCA Crim 3365.

Theft

7

APPROPRIATION

Key Principle
Appropriation is "any assumption by a person of the rights of an owner ... and this includes, where he has come by the property (innocently or not) without stealing it, any later assumption of a right to it by keeping or dealing with it as owner". (**Theft Act 1968** s.3(1)).

Key Principle
Appropriation is established by the assumption of any one right of an owner.

> R. v MORRIS 1984
> The defendant swapped price labels on supermarket goods. On appeal against conviction for theft, the question was whether appropriation required an assumption of all of the rights of an owner or whether it was sufficient to assume just one right.

Held
❖ (HL) Appeal dismissed. It was sufficient to prove an assumption of any of the rights. [1984] A.C. 320.

Commentary
(1) Acts such as touching or moving goods may therefore be appropriation. However, obiter, the House limited its scope by requiring that it be an unauthorised act ("an adverse interference"). This requirement has now been overturned by *DPP v Gomez* (1993) (see p.70).

(2) Later assumptions of rights by those who have acquired property as bona fide purchasers for value do not give rise to theft if they are the rights the purchaser believed s/he had acquired: **Theft Act 1968** s.3(2)

Key Principle

Appropriation can occur even though the act is expressly or impliedly authorised or consented to by the owner.

> **LAWRENCE V METROPOLITAN POLICE COMMISSIONER 1972**
> A taxi driver overcharged a passenger (who understood little English). He falsely stated that the offered fare was insufficient and took further monies from the wallet that the passenger held open to him. He was convicted of theft and appealed on the basis that consent prevented liability.

Held

❖ (HL) Appeal dismissed. The facts probably did not establish consent but, in any event, the prosecution did not have to prove that the taking was without consent. [1972] A.C. 626.

Commentary

Despite various attempts at reconciliation, there seemed to be a conflict between *Lawrence* and the view in *Morris* that appropriation involves "not an act expressly or impliedly authorised by the owner". Nevertheless, in *Morris*, Lord Roskill agreed that *Lawrence* was rightly decided. He also approved *R. v Skipp* (1975) (CA), where appropriation did not occur until the defendant did an unauthorised act of diverting from his delivery route and *Eddy v Niman* (1981) (DC), where would-be shoplifters were not guilty of theft having done no more than put goods into shop trolleys (authorised acts). The matter has now been resolved in the next case.

> **DPP V GOMEZ 1993**
> The defendant obtained authority for transactions by falsely representing that stolen cheques were genuine. His conviction for theft of the goods was quashed following *Morris* and the Crown appealed.

Held

❖ (HL) Appeal allowed. It was not possible to reconcile *Morris* and *Lawrence*. *Morris* was incorrect and *Lawrence* should be followed. Therefore the defendant was guilty because appropriation occurred despite consent. [1993] A.C. 442.

Commentary

(1) The decision in *Morris* that the assumption of any right amounts to appropriation was approved. Combined with the fact that this can now be consensual or authorised, theft widens yet further in scope because, for

example, touching goods on a shop-shelf may now be appropriation. Appropriation may also occur in conflict with the civil law position on rights in property. See *R. v Hinks* (2001) below.

(2) *Skipp* was overruled. Presumably, *Eddy v Niman* is also incorrect because, following obiter in *Gomez*, putting goods in a shop trolley may be appropriation.

Key Principle
Appropriation can occur even where the defendant thereby acquires an indefeasible title to the property.

> R. V HINKS 2001
> The defendant received property (in excess of £60,000) from a man of limited intelligence. She was convicted of theft and appealed on the basis that, inter alia, she had been given the property as a gift. Since the man was, despite his limited intelligence, capable of making a valid gift, title had passed to her and there could be no theft.

Held
❖ (HL) Appeal dismissed. The definition of appropriation laid down in *DPP v Gomez* (1993) included indefeasible gifts of property. A donee of a valid gift could be said to have appropriated the gift and, if dishonest, may be guilty of theft. [2001] 2 A.C. 241.

Commentary
(1) This decision applies *DPP v Gomez* (1993) in that Hinks appropriated even though the victim had consented to parting with the property. However, it also creates a possible conflict with civil law because she was convicted of stealing property that she arguably was entitled to keep in civil law, having acquired title to it.

(2) The case also clarifies earlier doubts (see for example *R. v Mazo* (1997)) about whether the decision in *DPP v Gomez* (1993) was restricted to situations where consent was obtained by deception. There is no such restriction on its operation.

Key Principle

If property is stolen once, it cannot be appropriated again by the same person exercising rights over it.

> R. v ATAKPU 1993
>
> The defendants hired vehicles abroad by deception and delivered them to Dover, intending to ring and sell them in England. They were convicted of conspiracy to steal (which required proof that the cars were stolen in England).

Held

❖ (CA) Defendants' appeal allowed. By virtue of *Gomez*, the obtaining of the cars abroad by deception was also theft. Since it was not possible for the stolen cars to be stolen again by the same thieves, there was no theft in England. [1993] 4 All E.R. 215.

Commentary

The **Theft Act 1968** s.3 says that a later assumption amounts to appropriation where the person has "come by the property ... without stealing it". This precluded the possibility of appropriation by the same person's later assumption of property already acquired by theft.

Key Principle

Appropriation can be a continuous act, but only for as long as the defendant is acting in the course of the same transaction.

> R. v ATAKPU 1993
> (see above).

Held

❖ (CA) The second ground for allowing the appeal was that the theft abroad did not continue in England (by retention after the hire period or by ringing the cars). The court agreed that appropriation can occur instantaneously (*R. v Pitham & Hehl* (1976) see below and Ch.8, p.95) or it can continue for as long as "the thief can sensibly be regarded as in the act of stealing" (*R. v Hale* (1978), see Ch.8, p.87). However, it could not be said that theft of the cars continued for days after they had first been taken. [1993] 4 All E.R. 215.

Key Principle

Appropriation can occur without coming into possession or contact with the property.

> **R. v PITHAM & HEHL 1976**
>
> The two defendants bought furniture from M (to whom it did not belong) and arrived to collect it. They were convicted of handling stolen goods and appealed. The question turned on whether M had stolen the furniture before the defendants "handled".

Held

❖ (CA) Appeal dismissed. M assumed the rights of an owner by inviting the defendants to buy the furniture. The appropriation was complete on the offer to sell and so the defendants had handled stolen goods. (1976) 65 Cr.App.R. 45.

PROPERTY

Key Principle

" 'Property' includes money and all other property, real or personal, including things in action and other intangible property." (**Theft Act 1968** s.4).

Commentary

Subsections of s.4 explain in detail when land or things forming part of the land: s.4(2); mushrooms, flowers, fruit or foliage: s.4(4), and wild creatures: s.4(3) can be stolen.

Key Principle

"Money" in a bank account in credit or within an overdraft facility is a "thing in action", capable of being stolen.

> **R. v KOHN 1979**
>
> An accountant used company cheques to draw money from company bank accounts for himself. In some transactions the account was in credit. In others, it was in overdraft within an overdraft facility limit. In others still, it was in overdraft in excess of the limit. The defendant appealed against conviction for theft of the cheques and from the accounts.

THEFT

Held

❖ (CA) Appeal dismissed in respect of stealing from the accounts in credit and those within an overdraft facility. Where an account is in credit, the debt owed by the bank to the customer is a thing in action. A bank is also obliged to meet a cheque drawn on an account within its overdraft facility. This obligation is also a thing in action, capable of being stolen. (1979) 69 Cr.App.R. 395.

Commentary

The court said that appropriation did not occur "until the transaction has gone through to completion". However, since *Morris* and *Gomez*, the offence can occur earlier by simply presenting a cheque. This is confirmed in *R. v Williams (Roy)* (2001), where the Court of Appeal held that presenting a cheque which reduced the victim's credit balance in a bank account amounted to appropriation of that balance (property belonging to the victim). However, where the defendant has no direct control over the account but causes another (for example, the victim) to effect a money transfer there is no appropriation by the defendant: *R. v Naviede* (1997) and *R. v Briggs* (2003).

Key Principle

There is no property capable of being appropriated where a bank account is overdrawn without (or in excess of) an overdraft facility.

R. v KOHN 1979
(see p.73).

Held

❖ (CA) Appeal allowed in respect of stealing from the accounts overdrawn beyond the agreed overdraft limit. No relationship of debtor/creditor arose and the bank had no obligation to meet cheques drawn on these accounts. Therefore there was no thing in action, capable of being stolen. (1979) 69 Cr.App.R. 395.

R. v NAVVABI 1986
The defendant used cheque cards, obliging a bank to honour cheques when there were insufficient funds in the account and no overdraft facility. He was convicted of theft from the bank.

Held ....

❖ (CA) Defendant's appeal allowed. There was no appropriation of identifiable property in which the bank had rights. By using the card, the defendant had done nothing that assumed any rights of the bank to part of its funds. [1986] 3 All E.R 102.

Commentary ....

The appropriate charge on such facts would now be one of fraud, contrary to s.1 of the Fraud Act 2006 (see Ch.9).

Key Principle ....

A cheque is two separate types of property capable of being stolen: a piece of paper and a thing of action.

> R. v Duru 1973
> The defendants were convicted of obtaining property (cheques) from the GLC by deception (false mortgage application details).

Held ....

❖ (CA) Dismissing the appeal, it was established that the cheques were pieces of paper (the cheque form—personal property) and the money represented by the cheque (a thing in action—a legal right to sue on the cheque). [1973] 3 All E.R. 715.

Commentary ....

Whilst it is agreed that cheques represent two forms of property, this case was problematic for two reasons. In relation to the things in action represented by the cheques, *R. v Preddy* (1996) overruled *Duru* because, on the facts, it is clear that these did not belong to another. They belonged to the defendants as payees. In relation to the cheques as pieces of paper, there is difficulty with the mens rea (see p.83). An alternative position that has been argued is that the cheques are property in the form of a "valuable security".

Key Principle ....

Confidential information is not property capable of being stolen.

> Oxford v Moss 1978
> A student "borrowed" an examination paper to obtain advanced knowledge of the questions. He was charged with stealing the

confidential information (the exam questions) and acquitted on the basis that this was not property capable of being stolen.

Held

❖ (DC) Prosecution appeal dismissed. Confidence is a right over property but not a form of intangible property for the purposes of theft. (1978) 68 Cr.App.R. 183.

Commentary

Some forms of intellectual property do fall within s.4 either as "intangible property" (for example a patent) or as a "thing in action" (for example a copyright or trade mark). However, by analogy with *Oxford v Moss*, a trade secret is not property.

BELONGING TO ANOTHER

Key Principle

Property belongs "to any person having possession or control ... or ... any proprietary right or interest ...". (**Theft Act 1968** s.5(1)).

R. v MARSHALL, COOMBES & EREN 1998

The defendants appealed against conviction for theft of underground tickets obtained from passengers and sold at a reduced rate to other passengers.

Held

❖ (CA) Appeal dismissed. The tickets still belonged to London Underground because they retained a proprietary right or interest in them. (1998) 2 Cr.App.R. 282.

Commentary

The tickets were treated as tangible property rather than as the chose in action represented by the tickets. A second reason for holding that the tickets belonged to London Underground was the express term on the tickets to that effect.

Key Principle

Control of land may include control of articles on the land.

R. v WOODMAN 1974

The defendants were convicted of stealing scrap metal from a disused site owned by ECC. The site was surrounded by barbed wire and notices, declaring it to be private property and excluding trespassers.

Held

❖ (CA) Defendants' appeal dismissed. ECC demonstrated their control of the site by the steps taken to exclude others and were therefore also in control of articles on the site (whether or not they knew of their existence). [1974] 1 Q.B. 754.

Key Principle

A person with a proprietary right or interest can steal the property from another with possession or control.

R. v TURNER (NO.2) 1971

The defendant took his car from a garage without paying for repairs. He was convicted of stealing the car and appealed.

Held

❖ (CA) Appeal dismissed. The trial judge had been correct that, even in the absence of a lien over the car, the garage owner had possession and control of it so it could be stolen from him. [1971] 2 All E.R. 441.

Commentary

This has been criticised. Whilst the repairer's lien would give the garage a proprietary right over the car, possession or control did not, in civil law, give the garage a better right to the car than the bailor (Turner) who could retake the goods at any time. Compare *R. v Meredith* (1973) (no theft on removing a lawfully impounded car from police possession).

Key Principle

Property may belong to someone with an equitable right or interest (other than one "arising only from an agreement to transfer or grant an interest").

R. v SHADROKH-CIGARI 1988

The defendant used bank drafts drawn on money credited to an account by mistake. He was convicted of theft and appealed on the basis that the drafts belonged to him and not the bank.

Held

❖ (CA) Appeal dismissed. Applying *Chase Manhattan Bank v Israel-British Bank* (1981), a person paying money under mistake of fact retained an equitable interest in the money. Therefore, whilst the defendant had legal ownership of the drafts, the bank retained an equitable interest. The court also referred to s.5(4) (see below) as an alternative method for reaching the same decision. [1988] Crim. L.R. 465.

Commentary

The equitable interest arising in *Shadrokh* is, presumably, because the law imposes a constructive trust and so the decision in *Attorney-General's Reference (No.1 of 1985)* (see p.80) may now be doubted.

Key Principle

Generally, if possession, control and the proprietary right and interest in goods pass to the defendant before the appropriation, the property does not belong to another.

> DIP KAUR V CC FOR HAMPSHIRE 1981
> The defendant was convicted of theft of a pair of shoes. She took a pair which she knew cost £6.99 to the cashier. One was priced at £4.99, the other at £6.99 and the cashier charged £4.99 which the defendant paid.

Held

❖ (DC) Defendant's appeal allowed. Appropriation occurred when she took the shoes from the cashier, having paid the price charged. However, the cashier had acted within her authority and the mistake (which was not about the nature of the goods or identity of the buyer) was not fundamental and so only rendered the contract voidable. Therefore property passed under the contract and the shoes belonged to the defendant when she left the shop. [1981] 2 All E.R. 430.

Commentary

(1) The court stated that s.5(4) (see below) was inapplicable because, under a voidable contract, the defendant was under no obligation to restore the shoes unless or until the contract was avoided.

(2) If the mistake had been fundamental the contract would have been void and property would not have passed.

(3) Under *Gomez*, the defendant would probably be guilty because appropriation would occur earlier, whilst the shoes still belonged to the shop.

(4) For other examples of the importance in the timing of property passing see *Edwards v Ddin* (1976) and *R. v McHugh* (1976) (petrol put into a car); and *Corcoran v Whent* (1977) (eating a meal in a restaurant).

Key Principle
Property belongs to another under the **Theft Act 1968** s.5(3) "where a person receives property from or on account of another, and is under an obligation to the other to retain and deal with that property or its proceeds in a particular way".

Key Principle
Under s.5(3), there must be an arrangement giving rise to a legally enforceable obligation to deal with the specific property (or its proceeds) in a particular way.

> R. v HALL 1973
> A travel agent was convicted of theft of monies received for flights. He paid the money into the firm's account but did not arrange flights and could not refund the money.

Held
❖ (CA) Defendant's appeal allowed. The defendant was under a contractual obligation to book and pay for flights but there was no "special arrangement" that he retain or deal with that money (or its proceeds) in that particular way. Therefore, there was no obligation to do so and the money did not belong to another under s.5(3). [1973] 1 Q.B. 126.

Commentary
(1) A similar conclusion was reached in *DPP v Huskinson* (1988) (receipt of housing benefit payments). However, contrast *Wakeman v Farrar* (1974) where, on receipt of a duplicate DHSS Giro, the defendant was under an obligation, created by written agreement, to return the original if found.

(2) Also consider *R. v Wain* (1993) where money (or its proceeds) collected for the Telethon Trust, paid into a special bank account, was subject to a trust obligation to be dealt with in a particular way. But note the importance of correctly identifying in the charge the party to whom the property is deemed

to belong. In *R. v Dyke and Munro* (2001) the Court of Appeal allowed the defendant's appeal against conviction for stealing from the donors to a charity. The defendants were trustees of the charity and had appropriated money that had been collected from donors in the street. The Court held that, under s.5(3), the defendants were under an obligation to the beneficiaries of the trust (not the donors) to deal with the money in a particular way. They should therefore have been charged with stealing from the beneficiaries and not the donors.

Key Principle

Under s.5(3), the property must be received from or on account of another.

> ATTORNEY-GENERAL'S REFERENCE (No.1 OF 1985) 1986
> A manager of a public house had a contract with a brewery to only sell their goods and to pay the takings into their account. He bought beer from elsewhere to make a secret profit.

Held

❖ (CA) The profits were not received "on account of" the brewers. Whilst the defendant had breached his contract and was under an obligation to account to the brewers for the profit he had not received it on their account. [1986] Q.B. 491.

Commentary

Note the comment on this case at p.78. It might now be possible to argue that the situation gives rise to a constructive trust (which, even if, as stated in the case, does not fall within s.5(1) does mean that the profit is obtained "on account" of the beneficiary). Support is drawn from a civil case, *Attorney-General of Hong Kong v Reid* (1994) which holds that a person in a fiduciary position, receiving a bribe, holds the bribe on constructive trust. This would also affect *Powell v MacRae* (1977) which held that a bribe was not received "on account of" an employer.

Key Principle

Property belongs to another under the **Theft Act 1968** s.5(4) if received "by another's mistake" where the recipient is "under an obligation to make restoration (in whole or part) of the property or its proceeds or of the value thereof ...".

Key Principle

For s.5(4), there must be an obligation to make restoration.

> **ATTORNEY-GENERAL'S REFERENCE (NO.1 OF 1983) 1985**
> A policewoman's bank account was mistakenly credited by direct debit with wages to which she was not entitled.

Held

❖ (CA) Whilst the policewoman was not under an obligation to restore the thing in action, she was under an obligation to restore its value to her employers. Therefore failure to do so could amount to theft. [1985] Q.B. 182.

Commentary

Contrast *Dip Kaur* (see p.78). The obligation arose here under the civil law of restitution (unjust enrichment) due to the employer's mistake. A similar decision was reached in *R. v Davis* (1988) regarding the mistaken payment of a duplicate housing benefit cheque. *Chase Manhattan Bank* (1981) and *Shadrokh-Cigari* (1988) (see p.77) may now render the use of s.5(4) unnecessary in these cases because the payer may retain an equitable interest so that s.5(1) applies. Certainly where a mistake is fundamental, rendering a contract void, there is no need for s.5(4).

Key Principle

Under s.5(4), the obligation must be legally enforceable.

> **R. v GILKS 1972**
> The defendant was convicted of theft, having refused to return money mistakenly paid to him by a bookmaker.

Held

❖ (CA) Defendant's appeal dismissed. The money did not belong to another by virtue of s.5(4) because a gaming transaction is not legally enforceable and so the defendant was under no obligation to repay the money. However, because of the mistake, ownership of the money never passed to the defendant and so it belonged to another under s.5(1). [1972] 3 All E.R. 280.

Commentary

The ground on which the appeal was dismissed has been criticised as incorrect.

INTENTION OF PERMANENTLY DEPRIVING

Key Principle
Intention to permanently deprive is established if the defendant does not intend to return the specific property in question.

> ### R. v VELUMYL 1989
> The defendant took cash from his employer's safe, intending to repay the sum borrowed. He was convicted of theft.

Held
❖ (CA) Defendant's appeal dismissed. Intention to return objects of equivalent value might affect the issue of dishonesty but it established intention to permanently deprive of the original objects (the actual currency) taken. [1989] Crim. L.R. 299.

Key Principle
Under the **Theft Act 1968** s.6(1) intent is present (even without intent to cause permanent loss of the thing) if the intent is "to treat the thing" as one's own "to dispose of regardless of the other's rights".

> ### DPP v LAVENDER 1994
> The defendant used doors from council property to replace doors in another property, belonging to the same council.

Held
❖ (DC) The defendant had stolen the doors. His intention was to dispose of (deal with) the property regardless of the council's rights. He had therefore intended to treat them as his own. [1994] Crim. L.R. 297.

Commentary
(1) This was also the basis for rejecting the appeal in *R. v Marshall, Coombes & Eren* (1998) (see p.76). By re-selling the tickets, the defendants had an intention to treat them as their own to dispose of regardless of London Underground's rights. Another example of such an intention is illustrated in *R. v Raphael* (2008) where the defendants offered to return a car that they had taken from the victim if he paid for it.

(2) In *Lavender*, the court referred to *Chan Man-Sin v Attorney-General of Hong Kong* (1988) as authority for the proposition that "to dispose of" included "dealing with". For an alternative view, see *R. v Cahill* (1993) where the court accepted that it meant "to deal with definitely; to get rid of".

Key Principle
Intent is established where a defendant intends to return the thing once it has ceased, in substance, to be the same thing.

> **R. v DURU 1973**
> (see p.75). One of the grounds for appeal was that there was no intent to permanently deprive the GLC of the cheques.

Held
❖ (CA) Defendant's appeal dismissed. There was intent to permanently deprive of the cheques as things in action ("the right to receive payment"). Moreover, as a piece of paper, the cheque "changes its character completely once it is paid ... it ceases to be in substance, the same thing as it was before". [1973] 3 All E.R. 715.

Commentary
The mens rea in relation to the "things in action" is now irrelevant since *R. v Preddy* (1996) overruled this aspect of the case. In *Preddy*, the House of Lords also doubted that the mens rea was established in respect of the piece of paper (the cheque form) since this would be returned to the drawer. It is certainly true that the only change in character relates to the thing in action. As a piece of paper, the cheque form is still in substance what it was before. The suggestion that the cheque be treated as a valuable security might avoid these problems.

Key Principle
Under s.6(1), an intent is established in cases of borrowing or lending property if doing so "is for a period and in circumstances making it equivalent to an outright taking or disposal".

> **R. v LLOYD, BHUEE & ALI 1985**
> The defendants took films, made master video tape copies, returned the films and sold pirate video tape versions. They were convicted of conspiracy to steal the films which rested on proof of intent to permanently deprive of the films.

Held
❖ (CA) Defendants' appeal allowed. Under s.6, borrowing only suffices if the intent is "to return the 'thing' in a such a changed state that it can truly be

THEFT

83

said that all its goodness or virtue has gone". This could not be said because the films still retained their virtue and value on return. [1985] 3 W.L.R. 30.

Commentary
Because the films had not lost all their virtue, the borrowing was not equivalent to an outright taking or disposal.

DISHONESTY

Key Principle
A defendant is not dishonest if s/he believes s/he has a legal right to deprive the other of the property. (**Theft Act 1968** s.2(1)(a)).

Key Principle
A defendant is not dishonest if s/he believes s/he would have consent from the person to whom the property belongs if that person knew of the circumstances of the appropriation. (**Theft Act 1968** s.2(1)(b)).

Key Principle
A defendant is not dishonest if s/he believes that the person to whom the property belongs cannot be found by taking reasonable steps. (**Theft Act 1968** s.2(1)(c)).

Key Principle
Where the defendant does not claim a belief falling under **Theft Act 1968** s.2, the test for dishonesty is whether s/he realised that the conduct would be regarded as dishonest by ordinary people.

> R. v GHOSH 1982
> A surgeon claimed fees that he was not entitled to. He was convicted of obtaining property by deception on a direction that dishonesty was to be tested by contemporary standards.

Held
❖ (CA) Defendant's appeal dismissed. Since dishonesty describes a state of mind, it must be established subjectively. The question is whether "according to the ordinary standards of reasonable and honest people what was done was dishonest ... and if it was ... whether the defendant himself must have realised that what he was doing was by those standards dishonest". On that test, the defendant was dishonest and so despite the misdirection there was no miscarriage of justice. [1982] Q.B. 1053.

Commentary

The test of dishonesty is not purely subjective because a defendant is not judged by their own standard of honest behaviour but rather on their understanding of "ordinary" standards.

> **WHEATLEY V COMMISSIONER OF POLICE FOR THE VIRGIN ISLANDS 2006**
> The defendant, a government employee, was authorised to make and administer contracts up to a value of $60,000. He was required to get clearance to deal with any supplier in which he had an interest. Without obtaining clearance, he made contracts with two suppliers (in each of which he had a financial interest) the work being shared and the value of each contract being conveniently just under $60,000. The work was done and he authorised payments to each. He was held to be guilty of theft of the money. He appealed, arguing that there could be no dishonesty where a contract had been made and services rendered for an appropriate price. [2006] 1 W.L.R. 1683.

Held

❖ (PC) Appeal dismissed. There can be a theft without there being a victim who is the poorer as a result. The prospect of loss does not determine the issue of dishonesty. There was ample evidence of dishonesty in this case.

Commentary

(1) After this case it is clear that: (i) the wide definition of appropriation derived from *Lawrence, Gomez* and *Hinks* is firmly part of the law; and (ii) the *Ghosh* test of dishonesty applies in all cases other than the three situations where s.2(1) of the **Theft Act** states that there is no dishonesty.

(2) Just as loss to the victim is not a determinant of dishonesty, nor is the fact that the appropriation is made without a view to gain or for the thief's benefit: s.1(2).

THINK POINT

Do you agree with counsel for the appellant in *R. v Hinks* (2001) (see p.71) that "the effect of the decisions in *Lawrence* and *Gomez* is to reduce the actus reus of theft to 'vanishing point'"? Can you explain why this might be a serious objection to the decisions in those cases and in *Hinks* itself? In so doing, consider the test for dishonesty laid down in *R. v Ghosh* (1982) (at p.84) and the impact of article 6 of the **European Convention on Human Rights**.

Consider whether the defendant would be guilty of theft in the following cases:

(a) "S makes a .... gift to D because he believes that D has obtained a First. D has not and knows that S is acting under that misapprehension. (b) P sees D's painting and, thinking he is getting a bargain, offers D £100,000 for it. D realises that P thinks the painting is a Constable, but knows that it was painted by his sister and is worth no more than £100. He accepts P's offer." You can check to see what Lord Steyn thinks about these scenarios which are discussed in his judgment in *R. v Hinks* [2001] 2 A.C. 241 at p.251.

Consider the following example taken from *R v Ghosh* (1982): "A man .... comes from a country where public transport is free. On his first day here he travels on a bus. He gets off without paying. He never had any intention of paying." Do you think that the man is dishonest? You could check your answer against that of Lord Lane C.J. in *R. v Ghosh* [1982] QB 1053 at p.1063.

Other Offences Contrary to the Theft Acts

8

ROBBERY—THEFT ACT 1968 S.8

Key Principle

The defendant must use force on a person or seek to put a person in fear of force immediately before or at the time of stealing.

> **R. v HALE 1979**
> The defendant put his hand over a woman's mouth to prevent screaming whilst the other searched her house. The latter returned with jewellery and the defendants tied and gagged the woman to make their escape. The defendant was convicted and appealed against the direction that using force to effect an escape was sufficient for robbery.

Held

❖ (CA) Appeal dismissed. It was for the jury to decide, as matter of common sense, when the act of appropriation finished. Therefore it was open for them to decide that robbery occurred when the force was used immediately before or at the time of the theft, which still continued to the time that the victim was bound and gagged. (1978) 68 Cr.App.R. 415.

Commentary

(1) The actus reus and mens rea of theft must be established. In this case, appropriation was a continuing act (compare *R. v Pitham & Hehl* (1976) (see p.73) and *Atakpu* (see Ch.7, p.73)). *R. v Lockley* (1995) decided that *Gomez* (see Ch.7, p.70) had not affected *Hale* and appropriation could still be continuous so that the defendants were guilty of robbery when they used force after taking beer from an off-licence.

(2) The force must be used on a person and not just against property but the person need not be the one to whom the property belongs.

(3) A threat of force is also sufficient and it does not matter that the victim is, in fact, unafraid as long as the defendant seeks to create fear of force as in *B v DPP* (2007).

87

Key Principle
The meaning of "force" is to be left to the jury.

> **R. v DAWSON & JAMES 1976**
> The victim's wallet was stolen by one of three men whilst he was being jostled by the others. The defendant appealed against conviction for robbery on the basis that this was insufficient evidence of "force".

Held
❖ (CA) Appeal dismissed. "Force" has an ordinary meaning and was for a jury to decide. (1977) 64 Cr.App.R. 170.

Key Principle
The force or "threat" must be used in order to steal.

> **R. v DONAGHY 1981**
> The defendants threatened a minicab driver into taking them from Newmarket to London. Once they arrived, they stole his money.

Held
❖ (Crown Ct) The jury acquitted, following a direction that the threats must continue until the time of the theft and be used to obtain the money. [1981] Crim. L.R. 644.

Commentary
The jury may have decided either that the threat was too remote from the theft or that it was used to get the ride to London rather than "in order to steal".

BURGLARY — THEFT ACT 1968 S.9

Key Principle
The defendant must enter a building or part of a building.

> **R. v COLLINS 1973**
> The defendant appealed against conviction for burglary with intent to rape. He had entered the bedroom of a young woman who he believed to be inviting him in. There was evidence that he had intended to rape her if she did not consent but they had consensual sexual intercourse

until she realised that he was not her boyfriend, as she had thought. A crucial issue was whether the defendant had entered the bedroom via the window before or after the woman appeared to be inviting him in.

Held

❖ (CA) Appeal allowed for reasons discussed below. Edmund-Davies L.J. commented that the first element of burglary was that the defendant entered the building in an "effective and substantial" manner. [1973] Q.B. 100.

Commentary

(1) Whilst burglary still requires proof that the defendant entered a building or part of a building, the requirement that the entry be "effective and substantial" has been doubted: see *R. v Brown* (1985) and *R. v Ryan* (1996).

(2) The next case considers the meaning of "a building or part of a building".

R. v WALKINGTON 1979
The defendant was convicted of burglary with intent to steal, having been arrested in a department store, searching through a till, inside a three-sided counter. He appealed on the basis that he had not entered the store as a trespasser.

Held

❖ (CA) Appeal dismissed. The elements of s.9 included entry to part of a building. The physical partition of the counter was sufficient to mark it off as part of a building into which the defendant had entered. [1979] 2 All E.R. 716.

Commentary

The **Theft Act 1968** s.9 creates two offences: entry as a trespasser with ulterior intent (s.9(1)(a)) and entry as a trespasser and commission of an ulterior offence (s.9(1)(b)). Each offence is also divided into two offences, one where it is committed in a dwelling and the other where the building is not a dwelling. Burglary of a dwelling carries a maximum penalty of 14 years: s.9(3)(a); burglary of other buildings carries a maximum of 10 years: s.9(3)(b).

Key Principle
The entry must be "as a trespasser".

R. v WALKINGTON 1979
(see above).

Commentary

The case illustrates that whilst entry to the building may not be "as a trespasser", entry into a part of the building (the three-sided counter) for which one has no permission will suffice.

R. v JONES & SMITH 1976

The defendants entered Smith's father's house with intent to steal two televisions. They were convicted of burglary under s.9(1)(b) (on the basis of entering the house as trespassers and stealing therein). They claimed that Smith was not a trespasser because he had his father's permission to enter the house.

Held

❖ (CA) Appeal dismissed. Whilst a person with general permission to enter premises would not normally be a trespasser, entry with the intention of stealing once inside was entry in excess of permission and so trespass. [1976] 3 All E.R. 54.

Commentary

Both s.9 offences require that the defendant enter as a trespasser. The doctrine of trespass ab initio does not apply to burglary: *Collins*. Therefore exceeding one's licence after entry does not in itself make the entry a trespass. It was the criminal intention of the defendants on entry in *Jones* that destroyed the permission. This may be contrasted with *Collins* (discussed below). Note also that the implication from *Collins* is that permission to enter may come from the occupier or from the victim of the intended or ulterior offence.

Key Principle

The defendant must know that s/he is trespassing or be reckless as to the trespass.

R. v COLLINS 1973

(see p.88).

Held

❖ (CA) Appeal allowed due to a misdirection on the mens rea. The defendant must know that he is trespassing or be reckless as to the fact. If the defendant had already "entered" the window before believing that he was being invited in, he was guilty of burglary. If he had not yet entered, he was entitled to the defence that he had not trespassed because he believed that he had consent for entry. [1973] Q.B. 100.

Commentary
(1) Note that the mens rea must exist at the time of entry if s.9(1)(a) is charged whilst mens rea at any point during the commission of the ulterior offence satisfies s.9(1)(b).

(2) *Collins* was referred to in *Jones & Smith* where the court concluded that the boys were trespassers because they knew that they were entering in excess of the permission given. Whilst *Collins* deals with the mens rea of the offence, there is a problem in explaining why, like *Jones*, his criminal intent (to rape) did not destroy any permission to enter (in which case it could similarly be said that he knew he was entering in excess of permission). However, whilst the defendants in *Jones* knew that they were not given permission to enter to steal televisions, *Collins* may have believed that he was given permission to enter for sex (although he clearly was not given permission to enter to rape). There are other differences between the cases. The permission in *Collins* was specific—to enter for sex—whilst in *Jones* it was general—to use the house whenever. Moreover, the criminal intention in *Jones* is described as unconditional whilst that in *Collins* was conditional.

Key Principle
Under the **Theft Act 1968** s.9(1)(a) the entry must be with intent to steal, inflict grievous bodily harm or do unlawful criminal damage.

Commentary
The defendant must intend to commit the offence in question in the building entered as a trespasser. *Collins* and *Walkington* are examples of charges under this section. Rape was removed from the list of intended offences in s.9(1)(a) by the **Sexual Offences Act 2003**. Where the intended ulterior offence is rape, the appropriate charge would now be for the offence of trespass with intent to commit a sexual assault contrary to the **Sexual Offences Act 2003** s.63.

Key Principle
Under the **Theft Act 1968** s.9(1)(b), the defendant must commit the ulterior offence of theft, attempted theft, inflicting or attempting to inflict grievous bodily harm.

Commentary

Jones & Smith is an example of a charge under this section.

AGGRAVATED BURGLARY

Key Principle

The defendant must have a firearm, explosive or weapon of offence at the time of the burglary. (**Theft Act 1968** s.10).

> R. v FRANCIS 1982
> The defendants were armed with sticks, either just before or on entry to a building, which they then discarded. At the time of entry there was no criminal intent but after entry the defendants stole from the house. They were convicted of aggravated burglary on a direction that it was sufficient that they were armed on entry to the house.

Held

❖ (CA) Defendants' appeal allowed. The aggravating article must be present at the time of the burglary. The relevant time under s.9(1)(a), which did not apply on the facts, was at the point of entry. The relevant time under s.9(1)(b), which did apply, was at the time of the ulterior offence by which time the sticks had been discarded. [1982] Crim. L.R. 363.

Commentary

The meaning of firearm, explosive and weapon of offence are explained further in the **Theft Act 1968** s.10.

BLACKMAIL

Key Principle

The defendant must make a demand.

> R. v COLLISTER & WARHURST 1955
> Two police officers were charged with demanding money with menaces. One told the other, in the hearing of the victim, that the victim had been importuning him but implied that a report might not be filed. At a following meeting the victim was asked whether he had brought anything with him at which point he handed over money to the defendants.

Held

❖ (CCA) The trial judge had been correct to direct that there need not be an express demand. Demeanour and circumstances might make it possible to imply that a demand was being made (and being backed by threats). (1955) 39 Cr.App.R. 100.

Commentary

The offence is complete on making the demand (with menaces). It is not necessary that an oral demand actually be heard or a written one received: *Treacy v DPP* (1971).

Key Principle

The demand must be accompanied by menaces.

> R. v GARWOOD 1987
> The defendant was convicted of blackmail having made a demand of someone who was timid and more likely to feel menaced than an ordinary person. The judge directed that the victim's timidity did not prevent the finding of a menace.

Held

❖ (CA) Defendants' appeal dismissed. There had been a misdirection but no miscarriage of justice. Threats that might affect the ordinary stable person but which do not affect the victim can still be menaces. Where a threat affects the victim but might not affect a person of normal stability it must be shown that the defendant knew of the likely effect on the victim before it can be said to be a menace. [1987] 1 All E.R. 1032.

Key Principle

The demand must be unwarranted. It will be warranted if the defendant believes that there are reasonable grounds for making the demand and that menaces are a proper means for enforcing the demand.

> R. v HARVEY 1981
> The defendants were "swindled" in a cannabis deal by the victim. They kidnapped his wife and child and threatened them and the victim if their money was not returned. They were convicted of blackmail and appealed against a direction that the demand could not be warranted because the menaces involved threats to commit criminal acts.

Held

❖ (CA) Appeal dismissed although the direction was not strictly correct. The test was subjective and so the question was whether the defendants believed the menace to be a "proper" (lawful, not criminal) means for enforcing the demand. (1981) 72 Cr.App.R. 139.

Commentary

In this case, the defendants probably believed that they had reasonable grounds for making the demand but they failed to satisfy the latter part of the test.

Key Principle

The demand must be made with a view to gain or intent to cause loss.

> R. v BEVANS 1988
>
> The defendant, who suffered a painful medical condition, called a doctor. When he arrived, the defendant, armed with a gun, threatened to shoot him unless he gave a pain-killing injection. The defendant was convicted of blackmail and appealed on the basis that his actions had not been with intent to gain or cause loss.

Held

❖ (CA) Appeal dismissed. The **Theft Act 1968** s.34(2) specifies that the "gain" or "loss" must be in money or other property. The pain killing liquid was property that the defendant was aiming to gain and so the offence was established. (1988) 87 Cr.App.R. 64.

Commentary

The same definition of "gain" and "loss" appears in s.5 of the **Fraud Act 2006**, see p.102.

HANDLING STOLEN GOODS—THEFT ACT 1968 S.22

Key Principle

The goods must be stolen goods when handled.

> RE ATTORNEY-GENERAL'S REFERENCE (NO.1 OF 1974)
>
> Suspecting that goods in a car had been stolen, a police officer immobilised the car and waited for its driver who was then charged

with handling stolen goods. The trial judge directed an acquittal on the basis that the goods had been restored to the lawful possession or custody of the police officer and had therefore ceased to be stolen under the **Theft Act 1968** s.24(3).

Held

❖ (CA) Whether or not the goods ceased to be stolen depended on the state of mind of the police officer. If by immobilising the car, he intended to reduce the goods into his possession or control ("take charge of them so that they could not be removed"), they had ceased to be stolen. However, if he simply intended to prevent the driver from driving away before answering questions, he may not have reduced the goods into his possession or control and so they were still stolen. The trial judge had therefore incorrectly withdrawn the question of the purpose of the officer from the jury. [1974] 2 All E.R. 899.

Commentary

(1) Other cases on this point include *R. v King* (1938) and *Haughton v Smith* (1975). Goods also cease to be stolen if restored to the person from whom they were stolen.

(2) "Goods" has much the same meaning as for theft and "stolen" means having been the subject of theft, blackmail or fraud. They also include goods directly or indirectly representing stolen goods (see **Theft Act 1968** s.24(2)).

Key Principle

The goods must be handled "otherwise than in the course of stealing" (i.e. after they have been stolen).

R. v PITHAM & HEHL 1976
(see Ch.7, p.73).

Held

❖ (CA) Defendants'appeal dismissed. Since the appropriation (and theft) was complete on offering the furniture for sale, the actions of the defendants thereafter were not "in the course of stealing" and so could be handling. (1976) 65 Cr.App.R. 45.

Commentary

Much turns on the duration of appropriation (as in robbery). Here the court rejected the argument that appropriation continued until the furniture was loaded into the van, deciding instead that it was an "instantaneous" act. For other decisions on the issue in a different context see *Atakpu* (see Ch.7, p.72) and *Hale* (see p.87).

Key Principle

There are two offences of handling. The first consists of receiving or arranging to receive stolen goods.

R. v BLOXHAM 1983

The defendant bought a car which he did not know had been stolen. Discovering that it had, he sold it and was convicted of handling by undertaking or assisting in the disposal or realisation of the car for the benefit of the purchaser. He appealed on the basis that his acts had not been undertaken for the benefit of another.

Held

❖ (HL) Appeal allowed for reasons given below. Lord Bridge explained that the **Theft Act 1968** s.22 creates "two distinct offences" of handling, the first being receiving or arranging to receive. [1983] 1 A.C. 109.

Commentary

The first handling offence could not be charged because the defendant lacked mens rea when he received (bought) the car.

Key Principle

Receiving occurs when the defendant comes into possession or control of the goods.

R. v BROOK 1993

The defendant's wife found a bag containing stolen cheques and cards. She told the defendant what was in the bag and he suggested that they put it in his car whilst deciding what to do. He was convicted of handling by receiving and the issue on appeal related to the mens rea of the offence.

Held

❖ (CA) Appeal allowed for reasons given below. Receipt was complete on coming into possession (control) of the goods. This was when, knowing what was in the bag, the defendant told his wife to put it into the car. [1993] Crim. L.R. 455.

Key Principle

The second form of handling is by undertaking or assisting in the retention, removal, disposal or realisation of goods or arranging to do so. This must be done for the benefit of another.

> R. v Bloxham 1983
> (see p.96).

Held

❖ (HL) Defendant's appeal allowed. The second handling offence covers four activities committed in one of two ways: the defendant undertakes the activity for another's benefit or another undertakes the activity and is assisted by the defendant. The "other" is limited in the same way in both parts. A purchaser of stolen goods cannot be "another person" (for whose benefit an activity is undertaken) because the act of purchase does not fall into one of the four activities (retention, removal, disposal or realisation). Therefore, although a sale might be a disposal or realisation for the purchaser's benefit, it does not fall within the section. [1983] A.C. 109.

Commentary

The four activities are different: retention means "keep possession of … continue to have": *R. v Pitchley* (1972) (see below); removal means transporting or carrying; disposal covers getting rid of or transforming; and realisation is selling.

Key Principle

"Assisting in" retention, removal, disposal or realisation requires something done that helps or encourages for the purpose of enabling the specified activity.

> R. v Kanwar 1982
> The defendant lied to the police about stolen goods in her home in order to protect her husband who had stolen them.

Held

❖ (CA) Merely using stolen goods (or keeping them in the house) was not sufficient to amount to assisting in their retention. Concealing goods was sufficient and lying to the police amounted to assisting in retention for the benefit of her husband. [1982] 2 All E.R. 528.

Commentary

See also *R. v Pitchley* (1972) where, having received stolen money from his son without knowing it was stolen, the defendant paid it into a post office savings account. Having discovered that it was stolen, he left the money in the account which amounted to assisting in its retention for his son's benefit. This case, unlike *Kanwar*, appears to impose liability for assisting by omission.

> R. v COLEMAN 1986
> The defendant knew his wife had stolen money from her employers and this was used to cover their expenses and to purchase a flat. He was convicted of assisting in the disposal of the money.

Held

❖ (CA) Defendant's appeal allowed. Simply getting the benefit from the disposal did not amount to assisting in it which required proof of some act of encouragement, agreement or help. [1986] Crim. L.R. 56.

Key Principle

The mens rea (knowledge or belief that the goods are stolen and dishonesty) must exist at the time of the act alleged to be the handling.

> R. v BROOK 1993
> (see p.96).

Held

❖ (CA) Defendant's appeal allowed due to a misdirection relating to the timing of the mens rea. If charged with receiving, the mens rea must exist at the point of coming into possession (and not any time thereafter). Moreover, the test for belief that goods are stolen is subjective not objective. [1993] Crim. L.R. 455.

Commentary

Contrast handling by undertaking or assisting in the four activities where mens rea formed at any point during the continuance of doing so is sufficient. Knowledge or belief that the goods are stolen (and not mere suspicion) is required but this is satisfied where a defendant "shuts his eyes to the obvious": *Pitchley*. The doctrine of recent possession and the **Theft Act 1968** s.27(3) can assist in proof of mens rea.

Key Principle

It is also an offence to dishonestly retain a wrongful credit. (**Theft Amendment Act 1996**).

Commentary

Because an increased credit balance might not be stolen goods, the Act introduces s.24A to the 1968 Act to cover dishonestly failing to take reasonable steps to secure the cancellation of a wrongful credit. A credit to an account is wrongful to the extent that it derives from theft, blackmail, fraud or stolen goods.

THINK POINT

Can you explain why a different approach was taken in deciding whether appropriation was instantaneous or continuing in *R. v Hale* (1979) (at p.87) and in *R. v Pitham & Hehl* (1976) (at p.73)? Can you explain the relevance of this point to liability as principal offender for theft, robbery and handling stolen goods in the following scenario. D1 takes items from a display counter in a shop, intending to steal them. She wanders around the shop and passes the items to her friend, D2. D2 conceals the items in her bag and heads for the exit. D2 is approached by a store detective who asks to see what is in her bag. She pushes the store detective to the ground in order to escape. Note: You might wish to consider also liability as an accomplice in this scenario (see Ch.12).

In the previous scenario, might D1 and D2 be guilty of burglary if they had agreed to steal the items before they went shopping? Do you think that the decision in *R. v Jones & Smith* (1976) (at p.90) would apply or might it be distinguished?

Would D be guilty of blackmail if he threatened to tell the victim's husband about their affair unless the victim agreed to have sex with him again for old time's sake? Might the defendant be guilty of a sexual offence (Ch.5) if sex took place?

D is arrested when selling a stolen watch. Explain the relevance of the fact that (a) the watch was stolen two weeks previously or (b) that D has a previous conviction for theft two years previously.

Fraud, Obtaining Services and Making Off Without Payment

9

FRAUD BY REPRESENTATION (FRAUD ACT S.2): THE ACTUS REUS

Key Principle

The actus reus of fraud by representation involves making an untrue or misleading representation of fact, law or present intention. (Fraud Act 2006 s.2(2) and (3).

Commentary

The **Fraud Act 2006** repealed a number of offences in the **Theft Acts 1968** and **1978** which were offences of obtaining by deception, including the offences of obtaining property by deception and obtaining services by deception. In such offences the actus reus was not complete until the property or services were actually obtained. This is no longer required. Telling a lie now amounts to the actus reus. It will, of course, not amount to the offence unless the liar is also both dishonest and has the other elements of the mens rea. If s/he does have the mens rea, then as soon as s/he makes the false representation the offence is committed. The offence is thus committed before the person to whom it is addressed hears or reads it—indeed, even if that person never reads or hears it.

Key Principle

The representation can be express or implied. (**Fraud Act 2006** s.2(4)).

Commentary

(1) A statement can be expressly false or misleading or can, like conduct, imply a falsity. So, for example, a defendant who orders food or drink in a bar or restaurant, thereby makes an implied representation of intention to pay for the food or drink (or at least that it will be paid for by someone). If there is no

such intention, the actus reus of the crime is committed when the order is placed. If the defendant does have that intention but later before leaving decides not to pay, continuing to act with no relevant change of demeanour can amount to continuing or repeating the representation—a representation now rendered false by the change of mind: *DPP v Ray* (1974). In such a case, the actus reus is committed at the time of the change of mind. There is an overlap of offences here, since a charge would also lie for the offence of making off without payment if the defendant leaves without paying (see p.105).

(2) A defendant who presents a cheque, thereby makes the implied representation that the present state of affairs is such that the cheque will be met on its first future presentment: *Metropolitan Police Commissioner v Charles* (1976). If a cheque guarantee card is used in relation to the cheque, there is also an implied statement that the defendant is authorised (i.e. by the bank) to use the card on that transaction: *M.P.C. v Charles*. The same implied representation is made by someone using a credit card: *R v Lambie* (1981).

Key Principle
A representation may be regarded as made if it (or anything implying it) is submitted in any form to any system or device designed to receive, convey or respond to communications (with or without human intervention). (**Fraud Act 2006** s.2(5)).

Commentary
Under this principle, the following could amount to the actus reus of fraud: inserting a foreign coin into a self-service machine; using someone else's ticket at a machine granting entrance to a car park, cinema, club etc; entering someone else's password to gain access to his or her emails, bank account etc.; "phishing" (sending emails seeking bank details).

FRAUD BY REPRESENTATION (FRAUD ACT S.2): THE MENS REA

Key Principle
The mens rea requires proof of (i) dishonesty, (ii) an intention, by the false representation, to make a gain or to cause a loss or to expose another to a risk of loss and (iii) knowledge that the representation is or might be untrue or misleading. (**Fraud Act 2006** s.2).

Commentary

Dishonesty has the meaning set out in *Ghosh* (p.84). For the meaning of gain or loss etc., see the next key principle. Making false representations with the intention of making a gain is likely to be the commonest way of committing the offence, as where the defendant knowingly makes a false representation when: (i) applying for a job; (ii) making an insurance claim; (iii) selling goods; or (iv) asking for money.

Key Principle

In the offence of fraud, "gain" and "loss" extend only to gain or loss (temporary or permanent) in money or other property. Property includes real and personal property and things in action and other intangible property. "Gain" includes a gain by keeping what one has, as well as a gain by getting what one does not have. "Loss" includes a loss by not getting what one might get, as well as a loss by parting with what one has. (**Fraud Act 2006** s.5).

Commentary

Imagine X has lent Ben £100 until Ben receives his pay at the end of the month. At the end of the month, Ben lies to X "My employer has underpaid me" and asks X to agree to wait another month for repayment. This appears to amount to fraud; Ben intends to make a gain by keeping temporarily what he already has. See also commentary to **Fraud Act** s.11 (p.104). The definition of "gain" and "loss" is the same as that which applies to blackmail and which is stated in the **Theft Act 1968** s.34(2)(a) and it is important to remember that there does not have to be any actual gain or loss, it is simply enough that the defendant intends this.

FRAUD BY FAILING TO DISCLOSE INFORMATION (FRAUD ACT S.3)

Key Principle

The defendant commits the actus reus by failing to disclose to another person information which he is under a legal duty to disclose. (**Fraud Act 2006** s.3).

Commentary

Generally, the law does not impose a duty of disclosure. Thus someone who applies for a job or who offers to sell goods, is not under a legal duty to disclose facts which, if disclosed, might affect the success of the application or the offer. Of course, making a positive representation might well amount to fraud by representation. Thus a car seller who turns back the odometer or who disguises gaps in the bodywork with filler and paint may well be making an implied statement, causing the car to tell a lie about itself and may well be guilty of fraud by representation. On the other hand, merely failing to give information, e.g. that the car has had 14 previous owners, is no breach of a legal duty. One situation where the law does impose a legal duty of disclosure is when one applies for insurance (or to renew an insurance policy). In that case a failure to disclose a material fact (i.e. one which might influence a prudent insurance in deciding whether to insure and, if so, at what premium) will be a breach of a legal duty and, if accompanied by the necessary mens rea, will amount to fraud by failing to disclose information.

Key Principle

The mens rea for fraud by failing to disclose information requires proof of (i) dishonesty and (ii) an intention, by the failure to disclose, to make a gain or to cause a loss or to expose another to a risk of loss. (**Fraud Act 2006** s.3).

Commentary

Dishonesty has the meaning set out in *Ghosh* (p.85). For the meaning of gain or loss etc, see relevant key principle under fraud by representation above (p.102).

FRAUD BY ABUSE OF POSITION (FRAUD ACT S.4)

Key Principle

A person commits the actus reus if (i) he occupies a position in which he is expected to safeguard, or not to act against, the financial interests of another person, and (ii) he abuses that position by act or omission. (**Fraud Act 2006** s.4).

Commentary

An employee is generally expected to safeguard and not to act against the financial interests of his or her employer.

Key Principle

The mens rea for fraud by abuse of position requires proof of (i) dishonesty and (ii) an intention, by the abuse of position, to make a gain or to cause a loss or to expose another to a risk of loss. (**Fraud Act 2006** s.3).

Commentary

Dishonesty has the meaning set out in *Ghosh* (p.84). For the meaning of gain or loss etc., see relevant key principle under fraud by representation above (p.102).

OBTAINING SERVICES DISHONESTLY (FRAUD ACT S.11)

Key Principle

The offence consists of obtaining services (for oneself or for someone else) by a dishonest act and without any payment having been made for or in respect of them (or without payment having been made in full).

Key Principle

The offence is not committed unless the services are made available on the basis that payment has been, is being or will be made for or in respect of them.

Key Principle

The offence is not committed unless, at the time of the obtaining, the defendant, (i) knows that the services are (or might be) made available on the basis of the last key principle and (ii) intends that payment will not be made, or will not be made in full.

Commentary

This offence is intended to catch someone who by a dishonest act (usually telling a lie) obtains services which should be paid for but without paying for them—or not paying in full. For example, someone who is not an old age pensioner and who lies saying that he is a pensioner thereby gaining reduced price admission (e.g. to a cinema or theatre) would be guilty of this offence. What then of Bert, aged 58, who books himself in at an optician for an eye test, lying that he is over 60 when eye tests are free for those over 60. Bert is guilty of this offence only if the services he obtains are made available on the basis that payment has been or will be made for them. Bert's eye test was, however, made available on the basis that it would be free. The prosecution might well avoid this difficulty by charging Bert, not under s.11, but with fraud (by representation). Bert certainly appears to have the mens rea for fraud in that he clearly both is dishonest and also intends to make a gain by keeping what he already has (namely the money he would have had to pay for an eye test, if he told the truth about his age).

MAKING OFF WITHOUT PAYMENT (THEFT ACT 1978 S.3)

Key Principle
The defendant must make off (depart) from the spot where payment is expected or required for goods supplied or services done.

> **R. v Aziz 1993**
> The defendant refused to pay a taxi fare on arrival at his destination and so the driver was driving to a police station when the defendant ran off. He was convicted under s.3 and appealed on the basis that the spot where payment was expected or required was his destination and not from where he had made off.

Held
❖ (CA) Appeal dismissed. "Makes off" involves departing without paying from the place where payment is usually made, which varies from case to case. There was a making off on these facts. [1993] Crim. L.R. 708.

Commentary
In this case the making off was without payment for services done (the taxi ride) and the offence covers any legally enforceable provision of services such as the provision of hotel accommodation, *R. v Allen* (1985) (see p.107) and repairs done on a car, *R. v Hammond* (1982) (see p.106-7). It also covers the supply of goods, such as a meal in a restaurant, in which case, the "spot" varies according to the nature of the restaurant (it might, for example, be at the table or at the exit point).

Key Principle
The defendant must be required or expected to pay at the time of the making off.

> **R. v Vincent 2001**
> The defendant stayed in two hotels and left without paying the bills. He claimed that the proprietors of the hotels had agreed to postpone the

payment. The defendant appealed against conviction for making off without payment.

Held

❖ (CA) Appeal allowed. An arrangement to delay payment, made before payment is normally expected or required, prevents the offence from occurring. It made no difference whether the arrangement was obtained honestly or dishonestly. [2001] 1 W.L.R. 1172.

Commentary

Where the agreement is obtained dishonestly, a charge of fraud or of obtaining services by a dishonest act might be appropriate.

Key Principle

The expectation (or requirement) of payment must be legally enforceable.

> **TROUGHTON V METROPOLITAN POLICE COMMISSIONER 1987**
> A taxi driver was unable to get destination details from a drunken passenger and so drove to the nearest police station. The defendant was convicted of making off without payment of the fare and appealed.

Held

❖ (DC) Appeal allowed. The driver had breached the contract by not completing the journey. Therefore he was not legally entitled to require payment of the fare and so the defendant was not guilty. [1987] Crim. L.R. 138.

Key Principle

The defendant must make off without having paid. There is no such making off if a cheque is accepted in "payment".

> **R. V HAMMOND 1982**
> The defendant "paid" for repairs done on his car by a cheque that he knew would "bounce".

Held

❖ (Crown Ct) The defendant did not make off without payment because the garage accepted the cheque without a cheque guarantee card and allowed the defendant to leave. [1982] Crim. L.R. 611.

Commentary

This is a difficult case. Does it decide that the "consent" of the garage prevented a making off or is it that the cheque was "payment"? The judge distinguished the case of counterfeit money on the basis that the recipient does not know that s/he is taking a risk as s/he does with an unbacked cheque. This suggests that it is not the "allowing the defendant to leave" that prevents a making off, because that applies equally to counterfeit money. The difference is that counterfeit money is not legal tender but a cheque is. Therefore, it might be that a cheque (even a "dud" one) is treated as payment for the purposes of s.3. However, it is hard to see how a "dud" cheque is payment as "required or expected".

Key Principle

The defendant must intend to make permanent default.

> R. v ALLEN 1985
> The defendant left a hotel without paying his bill but claimed to intend to pay in due course. The Court of Appeal allowed his appeal against conviction and the Crown appealed.

Held

❖ (HL) Appeal dismissed. The reference to s.3 to "intent to avoid payment" means "intention to evade payment altogether". [1985] 1 A.C. 1029.

Commentary

The other elements to the mens rea of s.3 are knowledge that payment is expected or required and dishonesty (as defined in *Ghosh*).

THINK POINT

One objection to the decision in *R. v Gomez* (1993) (see Ch.7) was that it created an almost complete overlap between theft and the offence of obtaining property by deception (**Theft Act 1968** s.15) in cases where the victim had been deceived into parting with the property consensually. It was argued that Parliament would not have created the s.15 offence if it had intended this overlap. Does the creation of the new offences of fraud under the **Fraud Act 2006** dispose of this objection?

Under the old law, a teacher who had been appointed because she lied about her qualifications was found not guilty of obtaining property (her salary) by deception, contrary to **Theft Act 1968** s.15: *R. v Lewis* (1922). This was because the causal link was too remote as the salary was obtained by working and not by the deception. Do you think that this would be fraud under **Fraud Act 2006** s.2? In particular consider whether, in respect of the salary or the job, the defendant intended "by making the representation" to cause a loss or make a gain as defined by the Act.

The defendant takes a taxi to his destination where he runs off without paying. He never intended to pay. Consider whether the defendant could be guilty of fraud and/or obtaining services dishonestly and/or making off without payment.

Criminal Damage and Arson

. . . .
CRIMINAL DAMAGE ACT 1971 S.1(1)

Key Principle
Property belonging to another must be damaged or destroyed. "Damage" includes temporary impairment of property.

> HARDMAN V CC OF AVON AND SOMERSET 1986
> Members of CND were convicted of criminal damage having painted figures on a pavement in soluble whitewash. They appealed on the basis that there was no damage because the paint would wash away.

Held
❖ (Cr. Ct): Appeal dismissed. Damage covered "mischief done to property" and, having caused expense and inconvenience to the Local Authority in removing the graffiti, damage had been done. [1986] Crim. L.R. 330.

Commentary
(1) "Damage" covers not only permanent or temporary physical damage but also impairment of usefulness or value. See *R. v Whiteley* (1991) (below). Where the damage or destruction is caused by fire, it is arson by virtue of s.1(3).

(2) The property must belong to another: anyone with custody, control, a proprietary right or interest or charge on it: s.10(2).

Key Principle
The property damaged or destroyed must be tangible but the damage need not be tangible.

> R. V WHITELEY 1991
> A hacker gained access to an academic network and, inter alia, deleted and added files, left messages and changed passwords. He was convicted of damaging the computer discs and appealed on the basis that

destruction or alteration of information on discs was damage to intangible property (not covered by the Act).

Held

❖ (CA) Appeal dismissed. The damage done was intangible but the Act does not require tangible damage. The property damaged must be tangible which it was because he impaired the usefulness and value of the discs which were tangible property. The court also referred to the Computer Misuse Act 1990 which now creates an offence of (and excludes from criminal damage) unauthorised modification of computer material. (1991) 93 Cr.App.R. 25.

Commentary

Section 10(1) defines property in much the same way as for theft except that land can be the subject of criminal damage without exception and intangible property cannot. This case decides that damage to intangible property (for example data or computer programs) does not fall within the Act but is included if by so doing the defendant damages tangible property (for example discs).

Key Principle

The mens rea of criminal damage is satisfied by proof of intention or advertent recklessness.

R. v G 2003
(see Ch.2).

Held

❖ (HL) "A person acts ... 'recklessly' [within the meaning of s.1 of the 1971 Act] with respect to—

(i) a circumstance when he is aware of a risk that it exists or will exist;

(ii) a result when he is aware of a risk that it will occur;

and it is, in the circumstances known to him, unreasonable to take the risk... ". [2003] 4 All E.R. 765.

Commentary

This decision disposes of the objective test laid down in *R. v Caldwell* (1982). *Caldwell* had defined recklessness as including a failure to advert to an obvious risk. In confining recklessness to subjective advertence, the House of Lords has also disposed of decisions such as *Elliott v C* (1983) (see Ch.2), *Stephen (Malcolm R.)* (1984) and *R. v Sangha* (1988) (see below).

Key Principle

A defendant who concludes that there is no risk of damage does not commit criminal damage.

> ### CC OF AVON V SHIMMEN 1987
> (see Ch.2, p.21).

Commentary

The case confirms that realising a risk of damage but thinking that it has been minimised amounts to recklessness but mistakenly thinking that there is no risk at all does not.

Key Principle

Belief that the person entitled to consent to the damage or destruction had consented or would have done so if they had known of the circumstances amounts to lawful excuse. (**Criminal Damage Act 1971** s.5(2)(a)).

> ### R. V DENTON 1982
> The defendant set fire to machinery, having been asked by his employer to do so. He appealed against conviction for criminal damage.

Held

❖ (CA) Appeal allowed. Honest belief that his employer (the person entitled to consent) had consented amounted to a lawful excuse under Criminal **Damage Act 1971** s.5(2)(a). Moreover, since the owner had in fact consented, there was lawful excuse under s.1(1) even without recourse to s.5(2)(a). [1982] 1 All E.R. 65.

Commentary

The belief has to be honest but does not have to be based on reasonable grounds. Thus a defendant may rely on this belief where it is caused by self-induced intoxication: *Jaggard v Dickinson* (1981) (see Ch.13, p.144). Nevertheless, a belief, however genuine, that God consented to (or instructed one to do) the damage does not amount to lawful excuse: see *Blake v DPP* (1993) (DC) where a vicar unsuccessfully tried, inter alia, to use this defence, having written a Biblical quote on a pillar in protest about the use of military force in the Gulf.

Key Principle

A defendant has lawful excuse under s.5(2)(b), if the damage was done to protect other property that the defendant believed to be in immediate need of protection and in the belief that the means adopted were reasonable in the circumstances.

> ### R. v HILL & HALL 1989
> Members of CND were convicted under **Criminal Damage Act 1971** s.3 for being in possession of a hacksaw blade, intending to use it to cut through the perimeter fence of a US base. They claimed the lawful excuse that they were aiming to protect property in the UK from the risk of a nuclear strike by "persuading" the US to withdraw their base.

Held

❖ (CA) Application for leave to appeal refused. The defendants' belief was subjectively judged, but, on the facts as the defendant believed them to be, the action must be objectively capable of protecting property. It was not so here because the actions taken were too remote from that eventual aim. Moreover, the section requires that the defendant believes that the property is in immediate need of protection and there was no evidence that the defendants believed that the nuclear threat was immediate. (1989) 89 Cr.App.R. 74.

Commentary

(1) The same conclusion was reached in *Blake v DPP* (1993) (above) where the vicar also unsuccessfully pleaded that his actions were done to protect property in the Gulf States because the causal link was too remote.

(2) The "thing" to be protected under s.5(2)(b) must be property, so this defence did not extend to protecting a child in *R. v Baker & Wilkins* (1997) (see p.168).

CRIMINAL DAMAGE ACT 1971 S.1(2)

Key Principle

The "aggravated" offence under s.1(2) does not require proof of actual endangerment but requires proof of intent to endanger life or recklessness in relation to endangering life.

> ### R. v Sangha 1988
> The defendants caused a fire in a flat which was temporarily unoccupied. Moreover, because of the way the buildings were constructed there was no danger of the fire spreading to other flats. The defendants were convicted of criminal damage (arson) contrary to s.1(2) on the basis of recklessness as to whether life would be endangered. They appealed on the ground that (albeit unknown to them) there was no obvious risk of endangerment due to factors that prevented a risk from materialising.

Held

❖ (CA) Appeal dismissed. Section 1(2) did not require that an actual danger to life existed. It was sufficient that the defendants intended such a danger or were reckless about it. For reasons given below, the defendants had been reckless and so the offence was established. [1988] 2 All E.R. 385.

Commentary

This was a case of criminal damage contrary to s.1(2), committed by fire. Such cases are charged as arson: s.1(3). The finding of recklessness in *Sangha* was based on an application of the *R. v Caldwell* (1982) objective test for inadvertence. The question in the case was therefore whether the defendants had failed to give thought to a risk that would have been obvious to a reasonable person. The court held that such a person was not to be endowed with "expert knowledge" (about, for example, the construction of the flats). Therefore the defendants had been reckless using a purely objective test. This part of the decision is no longer correct since *R. v G* has dispensed with the concept of inadvertent recklessness.

Key Principle

The intent (or recklessness) must be that the damage or destruction of the property be the cause of the danger to life.

R. v STEER 1987

The victims were looking out of their bedroom window when the defendant shot at the window. He was charged with, inter alia, criminal damage with intent to endanger their lives or being reckless as to whether their lives would be endangered. His appeal was allowed by the Court of Appeal and the Crown appealed.

Held

❖ (HL) Appeal dismissed. It was not enough to show that the defendant intentionally or recklessly damaged property and intended that life be endangered or was reckless thereto. It was necessary to show that the intent was to endanger life by the damage or that the recklessness was as to whether life would be endangered by the damage. Here, the danger was caused by the shot and not by the damage to the property and so the defendant was rightly acquitted. [1987] 2 All E.R. 833.

THINK POINT

Do you think that a defendant who floods a police cell by blocking the toilet with a blanket commits criminal damage to either the cell or the blanket? The water is clean, the floor is waterproof, the blanket is reusable when dry. Read *R. v Fiak* [2005] EWCA Crim 2381 to check your answer.

How does the offence under s.1(2) of the **Criminal Damage Act 1971** differ from the offence under s.1(1). Remember to consider both the actus reus and mens rea when considering this question.

Inchoate Offences

11

ENCOURAGING OR ASSISTING AN OFFENCE (SERIOUS CRIME ACT 2007 SS.44, 45 AND 46)

Key Principle

The actus reus of all three offences under ss. 44-46 of the **Serious Crime Act 2007** is committed if the defendant does an act that is capable of encouraging or assisting the commission of an offence.

Commentary

(1) The **Serious Crime Act** abolishes the common law offence of incitement and replaces it with the crimes of encouraging or assisting offences. Encouraging includes threatening or putting under pressure (s. 65(1)) and assisting includes failing to discharge a duty and taking steps to reduce the chance of prosecution for the offence (s.65(2)).

(2) It is enough that the act is capable of encouraging or assisting so it does not actually have to do so and the ultimate offence does not have to be committed.

Key Principle

It is an offence to do an act capable of encouraging or assisting an offence with intent to encourage or assist its commission (**Serious Crime Act 2007 s.44**).

Commentary

Intention is not established just because encouragement or assistance was a foreseeable consequence (s.44(2)).

Key Principle

It is an offence to do an act capable of encouraging or assisting an offence in the belief that the offence will be committed and that the act will encourage or assist its commission (**Serious Crime Act 2007 s.45**).

Commentary

This offence would be charged where the defendant does not have the direct intent to encourage or assist the commission of the offence but believes that it will happen. So a defendant who didn't want the offence to be committed, but realised that it would be committed and that his/her acts would encourage or assist it could still be guilty.

Key Principle

It is an offence to do an act capable of encouraging or assisting one or more of a number of offences in the belief that one or more will be committed and that the act will encourage or assist the commission (**Serious Crime Act 2007** s.46).

Commentary

This offence covers situations where the defendant encourages or assists without being aware of which crime the principal might commit. It is sufficient that the defendant is aware of a range of offences.

Key Principle

If the offence encouraged or assisted requires proof of fault, the defendant must have the requisite state of mind or must believe or be reckless as to whether the person encouraged or assisted has that state of mind. (**Serious Crime Act 2007** s.47(5)(a)).

Commentary

So, for example, if the defendant is charged with doing an act capable of encouraging P to commit theft, the prosecution must prove that the defendant intended to encourage the commission of theft and foresaw or intended that P would act dishonestly with intent to permanently deprive or that the defendant had that state of mind personally.

Key Principle

If the offence encouraged or assisted requires proof of particular circumstances or consequences, the defendant must believe that these exist or be reckless as to whether they do. (**Serious Crime Act 2007** s.47(5)(b)).

Commentary

So, for example, if the defendant is charged with doing an act capable of assisting P to commit murder, the prosecution must prove that the defendant intended to assist the commission of murder and foresaw or intended that the victim would die. This can mean that the mens rea of the offences under the **Serious Crime Act** differs from the mens rea of the crime encouraged or assisted as in murder which is also satisfied by intent to cause grievous bodily harm but is not satisfied by recklessness as to death.

Key Principle

A defendant who is aware of circumstances that make it reasonable for him to act as he did is not guilty of the offences nor is a defendant who reasonably believed such circumstances existed. (**Serious Crime Act 2007** s.50)

Commentary

Factors to be taken into account in determining reasonableness include the seriousness of the anticipated offences, the purpose for which the defendant was acting, and any authority that the defendant claims to have for acting.

Key Principle

In the case of protective offences, a person who falls within the protected category cannot be guilty of the offences (**Serious Crime Act 2007** s.51))

ATTEMPT

Key Principle

The actus reus of attempt is established only if the defendant has done an act that is more than merely preparatory to the commission of the full offence.

R. v CAMPBELL 1991

The defendant, who admitted intending to rob a post office, was arrested just outside the post office door. He had been observed earlier "lurking around" the post office in motorcycle gear and wearing sunglasses as a form of disguise. He had in his possession a threatening note and imitation firearm. He was convicted of attempted robbery and appealed.

Held

❖ (CA) Appeal allowed. The acts undertaken were mere preparation. (1991) 93 Cr.App.R. 350.

Commentary

The court took the view that whilst each case was to be decided on its own facts, it was unlikely that a person could be said to have committed an attempt if he had not even "gained the place where he could ... carry out the offence".

> ### R. V JONES 1990
> The defendant bought guns, shortened one barrel and test-fired them. He packed various weapons in his bag and drove to where the victim was dropping his child at school. He got into the victim's car and asked him to drive, pointing at him the loaded sawn-off shotgun (with its safety catch on). The victim grabbed the gun and threw it out of the car. The defendant was convicted of attempted murder and appealed on the basis that there was no attempt because he had still to remove the safety catch from the gun, put his finger on the trigger and pull it before the full offence could be committed.

Held

❖ (CA) Appeal dismissed. Whilst the acts up to and including arrival at the school were only preparatory, getting into the car and pointing the gun was sufficient evidence of attempt. [1990] 1 W.L.R. 1057.

Commentary

According to *Campbell* and *Jones*, "more than merely preparatory" is a question of fact and it is not appropriate to refer to the pre-Criminal Attempts Act 1981 tests. Guidance is provided in *R. v Geddes* (1996) where the test was whether the defendant actually tried to commit the crime (kidnapping) or merely got ready or equipped to do so. The facts apparently suggested the latter. *R. v Tosti* (1997) provides that acts of preparation are capable of being attempts if they are more than "merely" preparation. Applying the guidance from *Geddes*, examining a padlock of a barn at night, with a car and oxyacetylene equipment hidden nearby, was sufficient evidence of attempted burglary.

Key Principle

The mens rea of attempt requires proof that the defendant intended to bring about any results specified in the full offence.

> ### R. v WHYBROW 1951
> The defendant connected an electrical device to a bath, causing his wife to receive an electric shock. He was convicted of attempted murder and appealed against the direction that intention to cause grievous bodily harm was sufficient mens rea for attempted murder.

Held

❖ (CA) Appeal dismissed. There had been a misdirection but no miscarriage of justice. Whilst murder is satisfied by proof of intent to cause grievous bodily harm, attempted murder is only satisfied by proof of intention to bring about the full offence (i.e. intention to kill). (1951) 35 Cr.App.R. 141.

Commentary

Whilst the case is decided on the common law, the same principle applies to statutory attempt: *R. v Millard & Vernon* (1987) (see next principle).

Key Principle

Even where the full offence is satisfied by proof of recklessness in respect of a result, attempting the offence requires proof of intent.

> ### R. v MILLARD & VERNON 1987
> The defendants were convicted of attempted criminal damage on a direction that recklessness as to the risk of damage was sufficient.

Held

❖ (CA) Defendants' appeal allowed. The **Criminal Attempts Act 1981** requires proof of intent to commit the full offence. This is the position even where the substantive offence is satisfied by proof of recklessness in respect of a result such as "damage" in the case of criminal damage. [1987] Crim. L.R. 393.

Commentary

Even prior to *Moloney* (see Ch.2), attempt required proof of direct intent (aim/purpose) in respect of results: *R. v Mohan* (1976). Foresight was not equivalent to intent. The same is true under the Act: *R. v Pearman* (1984) although the *Woollin* direction will now apply.

Key Principle

Where the full offence is satisfied by recklessness in respect of elements (other than any specified result), recklessness in respect of those elements is also sufficient for attempting the offence.

> ### R. v KHAN 1990
> The defendants were convicted of attempted rape on a direction that recklessness as to lack of consent was sufficient mens rea. They appealed on the basis that attempt required proof of intent.

Held

❖ (CA) Appeal dismissed. The words "with intent to commit an offence" in **Criminal Attempts Act 1981** s.1 only apply to intent to do the act and to cause any results. Therefore, attempted rape required proof of an intent to have sexual intercourse. However, since recklessness as to lack of consent was sufficient for the full offence, the same is true for attempting the offence. [1990] 1 W.L.R. 813.

Commentary

Consider the effect of the **Sexual Offences Act 2003** on this decision.

> ### ATTORNEY-GENERAL'S REFERENCE (NO.3 OF 1992) 1994
> The defendants were acquitted of attempted aggravated arson, being reckless as to whether life would be endangered on a ruling that intent to endanger life had to be proven.

Held

❖ (CA) Intent had to be proven in respect of the result specified in the full offence (damage or destruction), but since recklessness in relation to endangerment of life was sufficient for the full offence it was also sufficient for attempting the offence. [1994] 2 All E.R. 121.

Commentary

The court also held that the *Caldwell* definition of recklessness applied as it did for the full offence. This is no longer correct in the light of *R. v G* (2003). Where knowledge is required for the full offence, knowledge must be established for attempting the offence.

Key Principle

Impossibility is no defence to a charge of attempting an offence.

The defendant was convicted of attempting to be knowingly involved in
dealing with a prohibited drug, having received a suitcase which he
mistakenly believed to contain drugs. He appealed on the basis that,
inter alia, impossibility provided a defence to the charge.

Held

❖ (HL) Appeal dismissed. Since the defendant had the mens rea and had
committed the actus reus of the attempt, he was guilty because **Criminal
Attempts Act 1981** s.1(2) provides that impossibility is no defence. The earlier
House of Lords decision in *Anderton v Ryan* (1985) was overruled. [1987] A.C. 1.

Commentary

The House of Lords decided in *Haughton v Smith* (1975) that legal impossibility was a defence to attempt (ratio) as was physical impossibility (obiter).
Criminal Attempts Act 1981 s.1(2) states that "a person may be guilty of
attempting to commit an offence ... even though the facts are such that the
commission of the offence is impossible". Nevertheless, in *Anderton v Ryan*,
the House decided that Mrs Ryan was not guilty of attempting to handle a
stolen video recorder when it could not be proven that it had been stolen.
They decided that s.1(2) merely abolished the defence of physical (or factual)
impossibility but had not affected cases of legal impossibility. *Shivpuri*
overrules this (although it could be distinguished because Shivpuri intended
to commit an offence—importing drugs—whilst Mrs Ryan did not—she merely
intended to buy a cheap video recorder). Lord Bridge stated that reasons
given to explain *Anderton* (the "doctrine" of "objective innocence" and that
of "dominant intention") were not to be used. In particular, the latter con-
tradicted s.1(3) of the Act which provides that a defendant's intention is to be
judged by reference to the facts as s/he believed them to be.

. . . .

CONSPIRACY: STATUTORY

Key Principle

The defendant must have agreed with one or more others that a course of
conduct shall be pursued which, if carried out in accordance with their
intentions, will necessarily amount to the commission of an offence, or would
do so but for the existence of facts making the commission of the offence
impossible.

R. v ANDERSON 1986

The defendant had agreed to participate in the planned escape of a prisoner. He had agreed to obtain wire-cutting equipment to be smuggled into the prison but claimed that he had believed the fulfilment of the plan (the escape of the prisoner) to be impossible and that he intended to take no further part in the scheme, after supplying the wire-cutting equipment. He appealed against his conviction for statutory conspiracy.

Held

❖ (HL) appeal dismissed. The mens rea required that the defendant intended to play some part in the agreed course of conduct in furtherance of the criminal purpose. It did not require that the defendant intended the full offence to be carried out. The defendant was thus guilty, since he intended to play some part in the agreed course of conduct. [1986] A.C.27.

Commentary

(1) Statutory conspiracy is defined in s.1(1) of the Criminal Law Act 1977. The rulings about this offence in this case have presented difficulties. For the requirement that the defendant intends to play some part in the agreed course of conduct, see *Siracusa* (below). The ruling that the statutory conspiracy did not require the defendant to intend the full offence to be carried out was not adopted in *Yip Chiu-Cheung v R.* (1995), where the Privy Council held that conspiracy requires an agreement to commit an unlawful act "with the intention of carrying it out".

(2) It has been held that an agreement to aid and abet another to commit an offence is not a statutory conspiracy because it is not an agreement that any of those party to the agreement will commit an offence (as principals). This was the case in *R. v Kenning* (2008) where the defendant sold hydrophonic equipment and cannabis seeds and was willing to aid and abet the growing of cannabis. His conviction for conspiracy to aid and abet the production of cannabis was quashed on appeal because it did not fall within the definition of statutory conspiracy. It might today be charged under s.44 of the Serious Crime Act 2007.

Key Principle

A defendant does not have to intend to play an active part in the course of conduct.

R. v Siracusa 1990

The defendant was charged with conspiracy to import heroin from Thailand and another conspiracy to import cannabis from Kashmir. He appealed, arguing that the judge had misdirected the jury as to the mens rea required.

Held

❖ (CA) Appeal dismissed. Participation in a conspiracy can be passive and an intention to participate (said in *Anderson* to be required) can be established by the defendant's failure to stop the unlawful activity. A conspiracy to import heroin (a class A drug) cannot be established by proof of an agreement to import cannabis (a class B drug at the relevant time). (1990) 90 Cr. App. R. 340.

Commentary

The ruling that participation can be passive was surely a way of getting round the ruling in *Anderson* that the defendant must intend to participate in the unlawful plan. Thus, simply intending that others will continue with the plan with knowledge that it involves a crime, will be sufficient. The other aspect of the decision in *Siracusa* was explained—and effectively watered down—in *Patel* (1991) and *Taylor* (2002). The result is that now the defendant will escape only if he mistakenly believed that the conspiracy related to a controlled drug of a class attracting a lesser maximum than the drug specified in the indictment.

Key Principle

Full mens rea as to circumstances is required on a charge of conspiracy. If the existence of a particular fact or circumstance is required for the commission of the substantive offence, then to be guilty of statutory conspiracy, the defendant must intend or know that that fact or circumstance shall or will exist when the conspiracy is to be carried into effect.

R. v Saik 2007

The defendant was charged with conspiracy to commit the offence of money laundering by converting bank notes. The substantive offence of money laundering (in s.93C(2) of the Criminal Justice Act 1988) required proof that the defendant knew or had reasonable grounds to suspect that the property represented the proceeds of crime. The defendant admitted that he suspected, but denied that he knew, that the bank notes were the proceeds of crime. He appealed against his conviction.

Held

❖ (HL) Appeal allowed and conviction quashed. Whereas suspicion that the money was the proceeds of crime would be sufficient on a charge of the substantive offence, knowledge of that fact was required for a conviction of conspiracy to commit that offence. That is the effect of s.2(1) of the **Criminal Law Act 1977**. [2007] 1 A.C. 18.

Commentary

Compare the position in attempted crime. Where recklessness as to a circumstance will suffice for the full offence, then it will also suffice on a charge of attempt: *R v Khan* (see p.120 above). *Saik* makes it clear that on a conspiracy charge only knowledge or intention as to circumstances of the full offence will suffice.

Key Principle

The conspirators' plan must be such that "if carried out in accordance with their intentions" it will "necessarily" involve the commission of an offence.

R. V JACKSON 1985

The defendants were convicted of conspiracy to pervert the course of justice by agreeing to injure their co-defendant if he was convicted at trial. They appealed on the basis that their agreement would not "necessarily" amount to or involve the commission of an offence (as required by **Criminal Law Act 1977** s.1) because the offence would only be committed if the "victim" was convicted.

Held

❖ (CA) Appeal dismissed. If the contingency arose, carrying out the plan would give rise to the commission of an offence. "Necessarily" did not mean inevitably. [1985] Crim. L.R. 442.

Commentary

The court in this case followed *Reed* (1982) where the defendants were held to be guilty of conspiring to aid and abet suicide. They had planned that one of them would visit individuals considering suicide and, having assessed them, would either give them faith healing, comfort etc. whilst discouraging suicide or else actively help them to commit suicide. That situation was, it was held, like the situation where A and B agree to rob a bank, if when they arrive it seems safe to do so. That agreement will necessarily involve the commission of a crime if it is carried out in accordance with their intentions.

CONSPIRACY: COMMON LAW

Key Principle

Common law conspiracy to defraud consists of agreeing to dishonestly deprive another of something (including injury to a proprietary right) or to dishonestly cause a public officer to act in contravention of duty.

> R. v Scott 1975
> The defendants were convicted of conspiracy to defraud by agreeing to borrow, copy and distribute films in breach of copyright. They appealed on the basis that they had not agreed to deceive anyone (such as the copyright owners).

Held

❖ (HL) Appeal dismissed. A conspiracy to defraud could arise without deception or deceit. To defraud was "to deprive a person of something which is his or to which he is or would or might be entitled and ... to injure some proprietary right of his ...". It was also possible to commit the offence without financial advantage being gained or loss caused. [1975] A.C. 819.

Commentary

The court also recognised conspiracy to defraud by causing public officers to act contrary to their duty. The offence requires proof of intention to defraud and dishonesty, but not intent to cause economic loss. Common law conspiracy to defraud is preserved by **Criminal Law Act 1977** s.5(2); and Criminal Justice Act 1987 s.12 provides that this may be charged even where the agreement is also a statutory conspiracy.

Key Principle

Conspiracy to corrupt public morals exists at common law where the conduct agreed upon would not amount to an offence by an individual acting alone.

SHAW V DPP 1962

The defendants published a "Ladies Directory" containing the contact details of prostitutes. They were convicted of, inter alia, conspiracy to corrupt public morals.

Held

❖ (HL) Defendants' appeal dismissed. The offence of conspiracy to corrupt public morals existed at common law. This might include conduct that was not in itself illegal but was calculated to corrupt the public morality. The jury were the arbitrators of what corrupted public morals. [1962] A.C. 220.

Commentary

The existence of the offence was confirmed in *Knuller v DPP* (1973) (see below) and is preserved by **Criminal Law Act 1977** s.5(3)(a). "Corrupting public morals" has been described as something that the jury considers to be "destructive of the very fabric of society": per Lord Simon in *Knuller*.

Key Principle

Conspiracy to outrage public decency exists at common law where the conduct agreed upon would not amount to an offence by an individual acting alone.

KNULLER V DPP 1973

The defendants published a magazine with advertisements for homosexual contacts. They appealed against conviction of conspiracy to corrupt public morals and conspiracy to outrage public decency.

Held

❖ (HL) Appeal dismissed in relation to conspiracy to corrupt public morals and allowed in respect of conspiracy to outrage public decency. A bare majority concluded that the latter offence existed at common law but there had been a misdirection on its elements. "To outrage" meant more than "to offend" or "to disgust" and public "decency" was a shifting standard. Moreover, according to Lord Simon, "public" decency means that the offence must be committed in public. [1973] A.C. 435.

Commentary

This offence is also preserved by **Criminal Law Act 1977** s.5(3)(b).

Key Principle

Impossibility is a defence to common law conspiracy to engage in a specific course of conduct.

> ### DPP v Nock & Alsford 1978
> The defendants were convicted of conspiracy to produce cocaine. They agreed to obtain cocaine from a particular powder in their possession which, unknown to them, would not produce cocaine.

Held

❖ (HL) Defendants' appeal allowed. Since the agreement was limited to engaging in a specific course of conduct from which it was impossible to commit the full offence, the defendants were not guilty. The answer might differ if the agreement had been of a general nature (for example, to go into the business of cocaine production) because this agreement would not be rendered impossible just because one powder would not yield cocaine. [1978] A.C. 979.

Commentary

Whilst this decision still represents the position at common law, statutory conspiracies are governed by **Criminal Attempts Act 1981** s.5 which provides that impossibility is no defence.

THINK POINT

In some circumstances, impossibility was a defence to the crime of incitement. Do you think it is a defence to the crimes that replace incitement (encouraging and assisting crime contrary to ss.44, 45 and 46 of the **Serious Crime Act 2007**)? It might assist you to look carefully at the definition of the actus reus of each of the crime.

Do you think that the changed definition of rape laid down in the **Sexual Offences Act 2003** has any effect on the decision in *R. v Khan* (1990) (see p.120)?

Can you explain whether the following would amount to conspiracy? The defendants agreed to sell (but not to use themselves) devices which, if fitted to an electricity meter, reversed the flow of current so that the meter recorded less units of electricity than actually consumed. The defendants were thereby agreeing to aid, abet, counsel or procure persons not party to the agreement to use the devices to deceive the electricity board. You can check your answer by reading *R. v Hollinshead* [1985] A.C. 975 (HL).

Parties

12

ACCOMPLICES

Key Principle
An accomplice is one who aids, abets, counsels or procures the commission of an offence.

> ATTORNEY-GENERAL'S REFERENCE (No.1 OF 1975)
> (see p.128).

Held
❖ (CA) Liability as an accomplice (secondary party) arises by aiding, abetting, counselling or procuring and these words probably differ in meaning. [1975] Q.B. 773.

Key Principle
Aiding and abetting requires proof of more than non-accidental presence. There must, in addition, be actual agreement, encouragement or assistance.

> R. v CLARKSON & CARROLL 1971
> The defendants watched a rape but there was no evidence that they agreed to or positively assisted in the crime. They were convicted of rape as aiders and abettors and appealed.

Held
❖ (CMAC) Appeal allowed. In the absence of prior agreement or positive physical assistance, mere presence was insufficient without actual encouragement and intention to encourage. [1971] 1 W.L.R. 1402.

Commentary
The court felt that mere presence might, in some circumstances, provide evidence of encouragement and intention to encourage. The next case is an example.

Key Principle

Evidence of encouragement may arise from a failure to prevent an offence if the defendant had a right to control the principal offender.

> DU CROS V LAMBOURNE 1907
> The owner of a car was convicted of driving at a dangerous speed, having failed to prevent the driver from doing so.

Held

❖ (DC) Defendant's appeal dismissed. As owner, he could and should have stopped the driver. Failing to do so when he had a right of control was evidence that he encouraged and approved the activity. [1907] 1 K.B. 40.

Commentary

Likewise, failing to act in breach of a duty to do so may provide evidence of aiding and abetting: *R. v Forman & Ford* (1988) (see p.133).

Key Principle

Counselling requires consensus but not causation. It is sufficient that the principal acts within the scope of the counselling.

> R. V CALHAEM 1985
> The defendant was charged with murder as counsellor and procurer, having hired a private detective to kill the victim. The detective did so, but in circumstances that suggested no substantial causal link between the counselling and the killing.

Held

❖ (CA) Defendant's appeal dismissed. The word "counsel" does not imply a causal connection. There must simply be contact between the offenders and a connection between the counselling and the offence. Since the killing was done within the scope of the counselling, liability was established. [1985] Q.B. 808.

Key Principle

Procuring does not require consensus but there must be a causal link between the offence and the procuring.

Held

❖ (CA) Whilst aiding, abetting and counselling probably require consensus,
the same was not true of procuring. Procuring "means to produce by
endeavour ... setting out to see that it happens and taking appropriate steps
to produce (it)". There must be a causal link in the sense that the offence
would not have been committed in the absence of the procuring. Therefore
the facts did raise a case of procuring. [1975] Q.B. 773.

Key Principle

An accomplice must intend to aid, abet, counsel or procure the offence. This
is satisfied by proof of voluntary involvement with knowledge of the
circumstances.

Held

❖ (DC) Appeal dismissed. Supplying "the instrument for a crime or anything
essential to its commission" amounts to aiding and abetting if done knowingly with intent to aid and abet. Proof of intent only requires an act of
involvement voluntarily done. [1959] 1 Q.B. 11.

Commentary

Intent does not mean desire or purpose and liability arises even where the
accomplice is indifferent about the commission of the offence. It is confirmed
in *R. v Bryce* (2004) that what is necessary is that "D did the act deliberately,
realising that it was capable of assisting the offence".

Key Principle

An accomplice must have more than a general criminal intention but need not
know the details of the offence to be committed.

R. v BAINBRIDGE 1960

The defendant was convicted as an accomplice, having supplied cutting equipment, knowing that it would be used for breaking and entering. He appealed on the basis that he did not know sufficient details of the planned offence to be an accomplice.

Held

❖ (CCA) Appeal dismissed. A defendant who only knows that an "illegal venture" is planned does not have sufficient mens rea. However, one who knows that a crime of the type in question is planned does have sufficient mens rea even though the details are not known. [1960] 1 Q.B. 129.

Key Principle

It is not necessary that the accomplice knows the type of crime to be committed as long as the crime falls within the range of crimes contemplated.

DPP FOR NORTHERN IRELAND v MAXWELL 1978

A member of the UVF was convicted in respect of driving to a planned bombing. He appealed on the basis that he did not know the nature of the activity to be carried out by the principals.

Held

❖ (HL) Appeal dismissed. Whilst the defendant did not know precisely what form the attack would take, he did contemplate a limited number of offences (including shooting, bombing and the use of an incendiary device). He was therefore guilty of whichever of these contemplated crimes actually occurred. [1978] 3 All E.R. 1140.

Commentary

Viscount Dilhorne and Lord Scarman rejected the criteria used in *Bainbridge* because liability should not rest on categorising activities into types of crimes.

Key Principle

It is not necessary to prove which party was principal and which was accomplice if the crime is committed in the course of a joint enterprise.

R. v Forman & Ford 1988

The victim was assaulted by one of two police officers in a cell. The defence submitted that, without evidence that the parties were acting in concert, the failure to identify who actually did the act was fatal.

Held

❖ (Crown Ct) Submission rejected. If it cannot be proved which party committed the assault, both must be acquitted unless there is evidence of joint enterprise in the sense that one did the act relying on the other's encouragement not to intervene or report the offence. [1988] Crim. L.R. 677.

Commentary

It was similarly stated in *Chan Wing-Siu v R.* (1985) (see p.134) that the prosecution does not have to prove who was principal or accomplice if the offence arises in the course of a pre-arranged plan or concerted action (joint enterprise).

Key Principle

Accomplices are liable for acts which they foresee as possibly arising in the course of a joint enterprise.

R. v Powell & English 1997

In *Powell* the joint enterprise was to purchase drugs. During the enterprise, the drug dealer was shot and killed by the principal, who Powell knew had a gun which might be used to kill or cause grievous bodily harm. Powell was convicted of murder.

Held

❖ (HL) Appeal dismissed. It is not necessary for the accomplice to have the same mens rea as is required to convict the principal offender. It is sufficient that the accomplice participates in the joint enterprise with foresight: (i) that the principal offender might commit the actus reus of the offence; and (ii) that the principal offender might do so with the requisite mens rea. [1997] 4 All E.R. 545.

Commentary

So, for example, it is not necessary that the accomplice intended death or grievous bodily harm for liability to arise in murder. It is sufficient that s/he realises that the principal might kill with this intent. This was said to be an application of the decision in the next case.

Key Principle

Where the act falls within the contemplation of the accomplice, the extent of liability depends on what the accomplice anticipated as a possible outcome of that act.

CHAN WING-SIU V R. 1985

The defendants were convicted of, inter alia, murder occurring in the course of a joint enterprise (armed robbery). The defendants appealed against conviction on the basis that they could only be liable if they foresaw death or grievous bodily harm would probably result.

Held

❖ (PC) Appeal dismissed. Liability arose because the acts occurred within the joint enterprise. Whether the liability was for murder or manslaughter depended on what the accomplice contemplated. If s/he thought that weapons would only be used to frighten, the crime was manslaughter. If s/he contemplated that they might be used to kill or cause grievous bodily harm, the crime was murder. It was not necessary that this be foreseen as probable, foreseeing that it might happen was sufficient. [1985] A.C. 168.

Commentary

(1) Because liability rests on each party's contemplation, an accomplice can be convicted of a more (or less) serious offence than the principal in respect of the same activity. This was confirmed in *R. v Howe* (1987) (see Ch.14). *R. v Roberts, Day (I) & Day (M)* (2001) is an example of a case where the accomplice was convicted of a lesser offence than the principal. The victim was killed in the course of a joint enterprise and the principal was convicted of murder. Although the principal's act (kicking the victim in the head) was contemplated by the accomplice, he had not foreseen the "murderous state of mind" of the principal. Therefore he could not be guilty of murder but was guilty of manslaughter based on having contemplated the infliction of some (not serious) bodily harm. Another similar example is *R. v Gilmour* (2000), which involved killing in the course of a joint enterprise to petrol bomb a house.

(2) *Chan Wing-Siu*, like *Powell & English*, confirms that it is not necessary to prove that the accomplice had the mens rea of the principal offence. However, *Chan Wing-Siu* and *R. v Hyde* (1991) decide that liability rests on what the accomplice foresaw that the principal might do, whilst *Powell & English* states that it also requires foresight of the principal's mens rea. See *R. v Rahman* (2008) for further discussion about this issue.

(3) The offence may be one of strict liability which thus does not require the principal offender to have had mens rea as to all the circumstances. Even so, an accomplice is liable only if s/he had foresight of the whole of the actus reus including the circumstances. Thus where the defendant allowed a friend to drive his car, he was not liable as a secondary party to dangerous driving unless he foresaw that the friend might drive dangerously: *Webster* (2006).

Key Principle

An accomplice is not liable for acts which fall outside a joint enterprise.

> ### R. v POWELL & ENGLISH 1997
>
> In *English*, the joint enterprise was to injure the victim with wooden posts. In the course of the attack, the principal stabbed and killed the victim with a knife which English may not have known he had. English was convicted of murder.

Held

❖ (HL) Appeal allowed. An accomplice cannot be liable for an act by the principal that is "fundamentally different" to that which the accomplice foresaw. Therefore if English did not foresee the use of a knife as a possibility, its actual use fell outside the scope of the joint enterprise. This meant that he could not be guilty of murder or manslaughter. [1997] 4 All E.R. 545.

Commentary

(1) Even where the accomplice has the relevant mens rea of a crime, s/he is not guilty if it occurs outside the joint enterprise (by an act not intended or foreseen by the accomplice). Much therefore turns on the precise scope of the enterprise. The House of Lords applied *R. v Anderson & Morris* (1966) (CA) that if one party "goes beyond what has been tacitly agreed as part of the common enterprise, his co-adventurer is not liable for the consequences of that unauthorised act"—though the House of Lords made it clear that the liability as an accomplice depends, not upon what s/he agreed to, or tacitly agreed to, but upon what s/he foresaw as possibly going to happen (discussed under next key principle). It is for the jury to decide whether the acts of the principal are fundamentally different from what was foreseen.

(2) The case also suggests that where a principal uses a weapon different from but equally dangerous to one contemplated, the accomplice may still be liable. This is explained further in *R. v Uddin* (1998) and *R. v Greatrex* (1998) where it was said that whether or not an action is outside the common

purpose is one of degree, so if it is of a "type entirely different" (*Uddin*) or "fundamentally different" (*Greatrex*), it may be outside the enterprise. The use of a weapon is one relevant factor in this test.

Key Principle

An act is not fundamentally different and does not fall outside the joint enterprise just because it is done with a more serious intent than was foreseen by the accomplice.

R. v RAHMAN 2008

The defendants were involved in a joint enterprise to cause grievous bodily harm to the victim who was attacked with a variety of weapons (baseball bats, a metal bar and a table leg). An unknown member of the group stabbed the victim who died from the knife wounds. The defendants were convicted of murder and appealed. They argued that the killing was outside the scope of the joint enterprise because it had been done with intent to kill which had not been foreseen by the defendants who had only foreseen intent to cause grievous bodily harm.

Held

❖ (HL) Appeal dismissed. An accomplice who foresaw a killing with intent to cause grievous bodily harm could be found guilty of murder even if the principal acted with intent to kill. An unforeseen intent to kill did not make a foreseen act fundamentally different. [2008] UKHL 45.

Commentary

The House of Lords indicated that an accomplice who realised that the principal might kill with intent to kill or cause grievous bodily harm would be guilty of murder unless (i) the principal used a weapon that the accomplice had not contemplated and which was more lethal than any that the accomplice had contemplated and (ii) for that reason the principal's act was fundamentally different.

Key Principle

An accomplice can only be convicted if the actus reus of the principal offence is committed.

Thornton v Mitchell 1940
A bus driver was acquitted of negligent driving but the bus conductor
(who was negligent) was convicted as an accomplice.

Held
❖ (DC) Defendant's appeal allowed. If the driver had not driven negligently
there was no act that the conductor could be said to have aided and abetted.
[1940] 1 All E.R. 339.

Key Principle
An accomplice can be convicted even though the principal is acquitted.

R. v Cogan & Leak 1976
Leak procured Cogan to have sexual intercourse with Mrs Leak without
her consent. Cogan was acquitted of rape because the jury accepted
that he believed Mrs Leak was consenting. Leak appealed against his
conviction for rape as an aider and abettor on the basis of Cogan's
acquittal.

Held
❖ (CA) Appeal dismissed. The actus reus of rape had taken place and that
was sufficient to convict an accomplice. It was no defence for Leak that Cogan
was acquitted due to lack of mens rea. [1976] 1 Q.B. 217.

Commentary
The same principle applies where the accomplice has committed the actus
reus but has a defence. A further example can be found in *DPP v K & C* (1997),
where two girls were convicted of procuring rape even though the principal
might have had the defence of doli incapax or lack of mens rea. The court
noted, obiter, that if the principal had been aged under 10, no actus reus
would have been committed and so the girls would not have been guilty.

Key Principle
A person who uses an innocent agent to commit the offence is guilty as
principal offender.

R. v Cogan & Leak 1976
(see above).

Held

❖ (CA) In the course of dismissing the appeal, Lawton L.J. indicated that Leak could have been indicted as a principal using Cogan (an innocent agent) as the means to procure the offence. [1976] Q.B. 217.

Commentary

This part of the judgment has been criticised on the basis that rape is an offence requiring personal action and cannot be committed by an agent. The same problem does not arise with offences where personal action is not specified.

Key Principle

An accomplice may avoid liability by effective withdrawal from the enterprise.

R. v BECERRA 1975

The principal committed murder in the course of a joint enterprise to use force during a burglary if necessary. One ground for appeal against conviction as an accomplice was that the defendant had withdrawn from the joint enterprise before the killing occurred.

Held

❖ (CA) Application dismissed. The defendant simply said "let's go" and then ran away just before the killing. Effective withdrawal varies according to the circumstances. By the time this defendant withdrew, he would have had to "repent" in a vastly different and more effective manner (by, for example, physically intervening to stop the stabbing or by warning the victim). (1976) 62 Cr.App.R. 212.

Commentary

Where possible, communication of withdrawal should be timely and give unequivocal notice that assistance and aid are withdrawn. So, in *R. v Baker* (1994) (CA), saying "I'm not doing it", passing a weapon back to another, and remaining at the scene was neither unequivocal nor effective withdrawal. Even in the case of spontaneous (i.e. not pre-planned) violence there must be something, such as walking away, to indicate withdrawal has taken place, as in *Mitchell* (1998) where the defendant simply threw down his weapon and walked off. Also consider the case of *R. v O'Flaherty, Ryan and Toussaint* (2004) which confirms that withdrawal is a question of fact and degree for the jury to decide upon. In this case, the evidence suggested that R and T had withdrawn from a joint enterprise involving spontaneous gang violence before the fatal blow was struck. R and T had participated in the violence at one location but had not pursued the victim to a second location where death was caused. Therefore R and T were not guilty of murder. O'F was guilty because the evidence suggested that he had not withdrawn. He had participated at the first location and then pursued the victim. Still armed with a cricket bat, he had been present (but not active) at the second location.

Key Principle

A person falling within the class for whose protection the offence exists cannot be an accomplice to it..

> R. v TYRRELL 1894
> The defendant was convicted of inciting the crime of having sex with her whilst she was under 16.

Held

❖ (CCCR): Defendant's appeal allowed. Since the purpose of the crime was to protect the girl it could not also lead to her being punished for an offence committed on herself. [1894] I Q.B. 710.

Commentary

The principle is limited to crimes where the person falls within the specific class protected by the crime. A person who is a victim in a looser sense can be an accomplice to the crime involved.

VICARIOUS LIABILITY

Key Principle

The language and object of some offences enables vicarious liability to arise for the acts of an agent or servant acting in the course of employment.

> COPPEN v MOORE (NO.2) 1898
> Despite contrary instruction from the employer, goods were sold by false description. The employer was liable vicariously.

Held

❖ (DC) Defendant's appeal dismissed. The effect of the relevant statute was to make masters or principals criminally liable for the acts of servants or agents committed within the scope of their employment. The defendant had therefore sold the goods through his servants. [1898] 2 Q.B. 306.

Commentary

(1) The "language, scope and object" of the statute enabled the imposition of vicarious liability which arose even though the acts were unauthorised. Other words that can be similarly construed include "use", "supply", "present" and "keep". Mens rea words cannot be extensively construed and so this principle can only be used for strict liability offences.

(2) The parties must, generally, be master and servant or agent and the act must occur in the scope of employment and not as a "frolic of the agent's own".

Key Principle

A person who delegates the performance of their duty to another will be held responsible for the actions and states of mind of that other.

ALLEN V WHITEHEAD 1930
Contrary to the licensee's instructions, the manager of a cafe allowed prostitutes to gather on the premises. The licensee was convicted of an offence under the Metropolitan Police Act 1839 which required proof of mens rea.

Held

❖ (DC) Since the defendant was absent from the premises and had delegated to a manager, that manager's acts and knowledge were imputed to the defendant. [1930] 1 K.B. 211.

Commentary

In reaching this conclusion, the court looked to the purpose of the Act and concluded that it would be rendered nugatory if licensees could avoid liability by absenting themselves from premises by appointing a delegate.

Key Principle

Whether delegation has taken place is a question of fact, requiring evidence of the transfer of authority.

VANE V YIANNOPOULLOS 1965

The licensee was in a restaurant basement when a sale in breach of licence took place elsewhere without his knowledge. The sale was by a waitress and the licensee was originally found guilty of knowingly making the sale in breach of licence.

Held

❖ (HL) Prosecution appeal dismissed. There was insufficient evidence of delegation on the facts. The waitress had not been "left in charge of the premises" and "all the effective management" had not been handed over. [1965] A.C. 486.

Commentary

The House of Lords expressed distaste for the principle of delegation. The defendant was acquitted because the court felt that delegation required a transfer of the whole of one's authority to another and some felt that it was necessary that the licensee be absent from the premises. However, compare the next case.

HOWKER V ROBINSON 1973

A barman made an illegal sale whilst the licensee was in a different bar. The licensee was found guilty of the breach of licence and appealed.

Held

❖ (DC) Appeal dismissed. Delegation was a question of fact and since the barman had been given complete control over the lounge bar, effective delegation had occurred. [1973] Q.B. 178.

Commentary

The decision was reached despite the presence of the licensee on the premises which the court said was not a conclusive factor. Moreover, delegation had taken place even though there had not been a transfer of all of the licensee's authority to the barman.

CORPORATE LIABILITY

Key Principle

A corporation is identified with its controllers (directing mind and will) such that their actions and states of mind are those of the corporation.

TESCO V NATTRASS 1972

A supermarket manager was responsible for an offence under the Trade Descriptions Act 1968. The Company was charged and pleaded a defence under the Act that the manager was "another person" for whom they were not liable. Liability turned on whether the manager was a servant (another person) or someone with whom the corporation could be identified.

Held

❖ (HL) Defendant's appeal allowed. A corporation is vicariously liable for the acts of servants in the same way as a natural employer. However, where the acts (and states of mind) are those of "the directing mind and will" of the company, liability is not vicarious. These persons are identified with the corporation, so that their acts and states of mind are those of the corporation. Because of the management structure of Tesco Ltd, store managers were not such persons and their acts were not acts of the company itself. [1972] A.C. 153.

Commentary

(1) The court referred to Denning L.J.'s description in *Bolton v Graham* (1957) (CA) that the "brain and nerve centre" of a company are identified with it whilst the "hands" of the company are not. The court said that normally it was the board of directors, managing director and other superior officers who carry out management functions whose actions are identified with the company. The Privy Council in *Meridian Global Funds Management Asia Ltd v Securities Commission* (1995) suggested a more flexible rule of attribution in a case involving a breach of securities legislation. The purpose of the statute was taken into account in deciding that the acts of officers who were for this purpose acting as the company could be attributed to the company.

(2) The identification principle allows the mens rea of an individual to be attributed to the company only if that individual is a director, the managing director or, possibly, some other senior official such as the company secretary. Thus in manslaughter by gross negligence, the company could not be convicted unless it could be shown that some such individual was himself or herself guilty of manslaughter by gross negligence: *Attorney General's Reference (No.2 of 1999)*. This made it very difficult to secure convictions against corporations for deaths which had occurred through corporate failings, e.g. in train crashes and ferry disasters. The Corporate Manslaughter and Corporate Homicide Act 2007 remedied this by abolishing any liability of corporations at common law for manslaughter by gross negligence and creating a statutory offence of corporate manslaughter. An organisation can

be guilty of this statutory offence if the way in which its activities are managed or organised (a) causes a person's death and (b) amounts to a gross breach of a relevant duty of care owed by the organisation to the deceased.

THINK POINT

Look back at the case of *R. v Rafferty* (2007) at p.8. Can you explain why the defendant was not responsible as an accomplice to the drowning carried out by the principal offenders?

Chan Wing-Siu v. R (1985) and *R. v Hyde* (1991) (see p.134) decide that the liability of an accomplice depends simply on his/her foresight of what the principal offender might do (the acts in question). On the other hand, *R. v Powell & English* (1997) (see p.133) states that it also depends on foresight that the principal has the requisite mens rea. Does *R. v Rahman* (2008) (see p.136) resolve this issue?

Can you explain how the vicarious and corporate liability of a corporation differ from one another?

Defences (1)

13

SELF-INDUCED INTOXICATION

Key Principle

Self-induced (voluntary) intoxication can be used as evidence to disprove the mens rea of specific but not basic intent crimes.

> **DPP v Majewski 1977**
> The defendant attacked a number of people but claimed lack of mens rea due to self-induced intoxication through drink and drugs. He was convicted of a variety of assaults on a direction that self-induced intoxication was no defence.

Held

❖ (HL) Defendant's appeal dismissed. Where a crime requires proof of specific intent, lack of mens rea due to self-induced intoxication results in an acquittal. However, it is a substantive rule of law that self-induced intoxication is irrelevant and no defence to a crime of basic intent (such as assault). [1977] A.C. 443.

Commentary

(1) The principles only apply to voluntary or self-induced intoxication (described as an intoxicant "consciously and deliberately" taken) and only where lack of mens rea is pleaded. If mens rea exists despite intoxication, the defendant is guilty as charged.

(2) There is a major difficulty in satisfactorily defining specific and basic intent crimes. Approval was given to Lord Simon's definition (from *DPP v Morgan* (1976)): a basic intent crime is one whose definition specifies mens rea that "does not go beyond the actus reus ... (the act and its consequences)". A specific (or ulterior) intent crime is one where the "mens rea goes beyond contemplation of the actus reus". It was also suggested in *Majewski* that a specific intent crime is one that requires proof of some "purposive element" and that a crime satisfied by proof of recklessness is one of basic intent. These definitions are not without difficulty. Examples of specific intent crimes given in *Majewski* were murder and s.18 of the

Offences Against the Person Act 1861 whilst assault, s.20, and manslaughter were crimes of basic intent.

(3) The court accepted that there was no logic in allowing the defence to a specific intent crime but not to one of basic intent. The House of Lords decided that s.8 of the Criminal Justice Act 1967 had no application in cases of voluntary intoxication and basic intent crimes. This suggests that evidence of intoxication turns basic intent crimes into strict liability so that the prosecution no longer have to prove the mens rea at the time of the actus reus. The reason given was that voluntary intoxication became an integral part of the crime, supplying the element of recklessness required in crimes of basic intent. This reasoning has also been the subject of much criticism (not least because of the problem of lack of contemporaneity). For an example of an alternative approach see the decision in *R. v Woods* (1981), where the Court of Appeal felt that evidence of voluntary intoxication was irrelevant but that the jury must still consider all the other evidence in order to decide whether the defendant was reckless.

(4) The principle established in *Majewski* has been held to apply only where the intoxication is through alcohol or "dangerous" drugs: see *R. v Hardie* (below).

(5) Crimes where the mens rea can be satisfied by proof of recklessness are crimes of basic intent—at least that is certainly so where the crime does not include any ulterior mens rea. In *Caldwell* (1982), Lord Edmund Davies expressed the view that aggravated criminal damage is an offence of specific intent. That offence can be established by proof that the defendant intentionally or recklessly damaged or destroyed property, being either intentional or reckless as to whether life was endangered thereby. This passage was cited in the next case.

R v HEARD 2007
The defendant undid his trousers, took his penis in his hand and rubbed it up and down the thigh of a police constable. He was convicted of sexual assault contrary to s.3(1) of the **Sexual Offences Act 2003,** which requires that the defendant "intentionally touches another person" and that the touching be sexual and without the latter's consent. He appealed arguing that his drunkenness accounted for him not having had the intention to touch and that since the mens rea did not include recklessness the crime was one of specific intent.

Held

Appeal dismissed. The Court of Appeal did not accept that the defendant lacked an intention to touch the constable with his penis. The Court went on to add that it is not open to someone charged with sexual assault to argue that his voluntary intoxication prevented him from intending to touch. The element of the offence requiring that the defendant "intentionally touches another person" is an element requiring no more than basic intent. [2007] 3 W.L.R. 475.

Commentary

So a crime which requires proof of a very specific intent is not a crime of specific intent. The case appears to endorse the view that basic intent is where the mens rea of the crime does not extend beyond the actus reus and has no purposive element beyond this. The same can be said, however, of the offence of murder, which is not a crime of basic intent. The Court in this case also observed that to flail about, stumble or barge around in an uncoordinated fashion, resulting in an unintentional touching, objectively sexual, would not amount to sexual assault—even if the reason for such conduct was the defendant's voluntary drunkenness. So, apparently, voluntary intoxication can be relied upon as evidence to show that conduct amounted to such an accident but not to show merely that the defendant lacked the intention to touch.

Key Principle

If the effect of an intoxicant is not common knowledge, the prosecution must prove that the defendant knew the risk of its effect before *Majewski* can be applied.

R. v HARDIE 1985

The defendant was convicted of arson being reckless as to whether life would be endangered. He claimed to lack mens rea due to the effect of valium which he had never used previously. He appealed against a direction that because the valium was taken voluntarily it could not negate the mens rea of the crime.

Held

❖ (CA) Appeal allowed. *Majewski* and *Caldwell* were based on the premise that using alcohol or hallucinogenic drugs is reckless because their effects are well-known. There is a difference between drugs known to cause aggressive or unpredictable behaviour and sedative or soporific drugs where such a presumption of recklessness is inappropriate. In the absence of evidence that it was generally known that valium might render one "aggressive or incapable of appreciating risks", the defendant could only be convicted if he himself appreciated this risk. [1985] 1 W.L.R. 64.

Commentary
The principle from *Hardie* does not apply where the effect of the intoxicant is common knowledge and the defendant simply does not know its strength: *R. v Allen* (1988) (CA) (a case involving homemade wine). Moreover, the outcome depends on the charge and the anticipated effect of the intoxicant. For example, the court opined that taking a soporific drug might be no defence to a charge of reckless driving.

Key Principle
Majewski applies only to pleas of lack of mens rea. In deciding whether self-induced intoxication can be used in support of a defence, regard must be given to the law relating to that defence.

JAGGARD V DICKINSON 1981
Whilst intoxicated, the defendant mistook a house for that of a friend. She broke a window to gain access and was charged with criminal damage. She pleaded a belief (**Criminal Damage Act 1971** under s.5(2)) that she would have consent for the damage from the person whose house she thought it was. She was convicted on the basis that such a belief, caused by self-induced intoxication, was no defence.

Held
❖ (DC) Defendant's appeal allowed. The distinction between specific and basic intent was only relevant to pleas of lack of mens rea and not to the issue of defences. Section 5(2) only required an honest belief and so even one induced by intoxication could be relied upon. [1981] Q.B. 527.

Commentary
Whilst the court accepted that the crime (s.1(1)) was one of basic intent, the defendant admitted an intention to damage property belonging to another and the only question related to the s.5 defence.

R. V O'GRADY 1987
The defendant was charged with murder and convicted of manslaughter after killing a friend following a drinking spree. He claimed

that the killing occurred in self-defence. He appealed on the basis that his defence should be judged not only on any mistaken belief in the existence of the attack, but also on any mistake about the severity of that attack.

Held

❖ (CA) Appeal dismissed. The defendant was not entitled, in any event, to rely on self-defence based on a mistake induced by voluntary intoxication. [1987] 1 Q.B. 995.

Commentary

The court held that the distinction between specific intent (murder) and basic intent (manslaughter) was irrelevant because mistake was a separate issue from intent. Self-defence was no defence when induced by an intoxicated mistake. The same reasoning was followed in *R. v O'Connor* (1991) (CA) (although the defendant's conviction for murder was reduced to manslaughter because his intoxication may have affected his mens rea). However, following *Williams* and *Beckford* (see Chapters 1, 2, 4 and 14), it is difficult to see why mistaken belief in self-defence is a separate issue from intent. According to these latter cases, such a plea is a denial of the mens rea of the crime charged which should mean that *Majewski* applies and the belief is relevant to a specific intent charge (for example murder) but not to a basic intent charge (for example manslaughter). Nevertheless, *O'Grady* and *O'Connor* were followed in *R. v Hatton* (2006) where the Court of Appeal held that in a murder trial it was not open to the defendant to rely, when seeking to establish the defence of self-defence, upon a mistake induced by his voluntary drunkenness. A similar principle is also laid down in the Criminal Justice and Immigration Act 2008 s.76(5) (see Chapter 14).

Key Principle

Where a defendant deliberately becomes intoxicated in order to commit a crime, s/he cannot plead lack of mens rea at the time of the crime caused by that intoxication.

ATTORNEY-GENERAL FOR NORTHERN IRELAND V GALLAGHER 1963

The defendant was an aggressive psychopath, a mental disorder with latent effects which could be brought on by alcohol. He killed his wife having formed the intent to do so and having, possibly, consumed alcohol to get the courage for the crime. In his defence, he pleaded insanity and intoxication.

Held

❖ (HL) Prosecution appeal allowed and murder conviction restored. If a person forms mens rea whilst sane and sober and then gets intoxicated in order to commit the crime, s/he has no defence, irrespective of whether the crime is one of specific or basic intent. [1963] A.C. 349.

Commentary

The case also dealt with insanity. Whilst a disease of the mind (such as delirium tremens) brought on by intoxication might give rise to a plea of insanity, this was not such a case. Here there was a disease of the mind (psychopathy) which did not cause a defect of reason nor prevent the defendant from forming mens rea. The intoxication then brought out a defect of reason but because he had previously formed mens rea, he could not rely on this self-induced defect of reason to plead insanity.

INVOLUNTARY INTOXICATION

Key Principle

Lack of mens rea due to involuntary intoxication is a defence to crimes of both specific and basic intent.

> ### R. V KINGSTON 1995
> The defendant committed acts of indecency which he claimed were due to him having been surreptitiously drugged. The judge directed that he could only be acquitted if the drugs caused lack of mens rea at the time of the crime. His appeal was allowed by the Court of Appeal and the DPP appealed.

Held

❖ (HL) Appeal allowed. The trial judge was correct. A defendant who had mens rea had no defence simply because involuntary intoxication caused him to lose control or to become less inhibited. However, where involuntary intoxication caused lack of mens rea it was a defence to any crime. [1995] 2 A.C. 355.

INFANCY

Key Principle

A child under the age of 10 is not criminally responsible. A child over the age of 10 may be found to be criminally responsible. (**Crime and Disorder Act 1998** s.34).

Commentary

Prior to the Act there was a presumption of doli incapax which applied to children between the ages of 10 and 14. This was a presumption that the child was incapable of committing a crime although this could be rebutted by evidence that the child knew that the act was wrong: *C v DPP* (1996) (HL). The Act has now abolished this presumption and has also abolished the defence according to the House of Lords in *R. v T* (2009). In this case, counsel for the 12-year-old defendant had argued that s.34 had merely abolished the presumption so that if a defendant under the age of 14 could show that s/he did not realise that the act was wrong the defence was still available.

INSANE AND NON-INSANE AUTOMATISM

Key Principle

A defendant is insane if suffering from a defect of reason, caused by a disease of the mind, so as not to know what s/he is doing or not to know that it is wrong.

> M'NAGHTEN'S CASE 1843
> The defendant suffered from delusions. He was charged with murder, having shot and killed Robert Peel's private secretary.

Held

❖ (HL) To be insane, it must be proved that "at the time of the committing of the act the party accused was labouring under such a defect of reason, from disease of the mind, as not to know the nature and quality of the act he was doing, or, if he did know it, that he did not know he was doing what was wrong." [1843-60] All E.R. 229.

Commentary

This test is known as the *M'Naghten* rules. The case also establishes the presumption of sanity.

Key Principle

A defect of reason requires deprivation of the power of reasoning and does not include retaining, but simply failing to use, powers of reasoning.

> ### R. v Clarke 1972
>
> The defendant, charged with shoplifting, pleaded lack of mens rea caused by confusion and absent-mindedness resulting from, inter alia, depression. The recorder ruled that the defence was insanity, because of the mental illness from which the lack of mens rea arose.

Held

❖ (CA) Defendant's appeal allowed. Whilst depression might amount to a disease of the mind, the defendant was not suffering from a defect of reason because she "retained her ordinary powers of reason but ... momentarily ... acted as she did by failing to concentrate properly ...". [1972] 1 All E.R. 219.

Key Principle

The defect of reason must cause the defendant either to not know the physical character of the act or not to know that it was contrary to the law.

> ### R. v Codere 1917
>
> The defendant killed a fellow soldier and was convicted of murder. The defence raised insanity.

Held

❖ (CA) The expression "nature and quality of the act" related to the physical character of the act (not its moral character). Moreover, "not knowing that the act was 'wrong'" meant "wrong in law" or "regarded as wrong by reasonable people". Therefore, a defendant who knew what he was doing and knew that it was contrary to the law was not insane even though he might not understand that the act was morally wrong. (1917) 12 Cr.App.R. 21.

Commentary

"Not knowing the nature and quality of an act" means that "he did not know what he was doing": *R. v Sullivan* (1984). Regarding knowledge that the act was wrong, a similar decision was reached in *R. v Windle* (1952), where the defendant was not insane because he recognised that his act was contrary to the law (even though he may have thought that it was justified).

DEFENCES (1)

Key Principle

A disease of the mind may be any curable or incurable physical or mental disease, of transitory or permanent effect.

> **R. v KEMP 1957**
> A devoted husband struck his wife with a hammer during a temporary lapse of consciousness caused by the effect of arteriosclerosis (hardening of the arteries). Since it was accepted that he did not know what he was doing due to a defect of reason, the only question was whether the cause of the defect fell within the definition of disease of the mind.

Held

❖ (Assize Ct) The defendant was insane because hardening of the arteries was a disease of the mind. The law does not distinguish between diseases of mental and physical origin. Either may amount to a disease of the mind if they bring about the relevant defect of reason. The condition of the brain is irrelevant as is the fact that the condition is curable or incurable, transitory or permanent. [1957] 1 Q.B. 399.

Commentary

Any disease that affects the "mental faculties of reason, memory and understanding" falls within the *M'Naghten* rules. The definition given in the case received approval in *Sullivan* (see p.150), subject to the important qualification imposed by *R. v Quick & Paddison* (1973) (see p.153).

Key Principle

"Any mental disorder which has manifested itself in violence and is prone to recur" may be a disease of the mind.

> **BRATTY v ATTORNEY-GENERAL FOR NORTHERN IRELAND 1963**
> The defendant was convicted of murder but claimed not to be conscious of his actions due to psychomotor epilepsy. He appealed on the basis that his defence of automatism should have been left to the jury.

Held

❖ (HL) Appeal dismissed for reasons given below. Lord Denning stated that not only were "major mental diseases ... such as schizophrenia ... clearly diseases of the mind" but so too were disorders falling within the definition given in the key principle above. [1963] A.C. 386.

Commentary

This definition was doubted in *Quick* (see below) and in *R. v Burgess* (1991) (see p.154), where it was said that a disease of the mind could exist even without a danger of recurrence. A disease of the mind can also exist without a violent manifestation.

Key Principle

To amount to a disease of the mind, the cause of the malfunctioning of the mind must be something other than an external factor of transitory effect.

> **R. v Quick & Paddison 1973**
> A diabetic nurse assaulted a patient during what might have been a hypoglycaemic lapse of consciousness caused by consuming alcohol and failing to eat after taking insulin. He pleaded guilty after the judge ruled that his defence, if any, amounted to insanity.

Held

❖ (CA) Defendant's appeal allowed. Any malfunction of his mind was not caused by "a bodily disorder" such as the diabetes. It was caused by external factors (namely insulin, drinking and failing to eat regularly) and so did not amount to insanity. "A malfunctioning of the mind of transitory effect caused by the application to the body of some external factor . . . cannot fairly be said to be due to disease." [1973] Q.B. 910.

Commentary

The appropriate defence was automatism. The court felt that the width of the definitions of disease of the mind given in *Kemp* and *Bratty v Attorney-General for Northern Ireland* (1963) (see above) might lead to unacceptable results if not restricted to internal factors. The dichotomy between internal and external cause has produced surprising results. In *R. v Sullivan* (1984) a man of "blameless reputation" involuntarily caused grievous bodily harm by automatic movements during an epileptic seizure. Adopting *Kemp*, the House of Lords ruled that the defence was insanity because it did not matter whether the impairment was organic or functional, permanent, transitory or intermittent. The position would differ if the impairment had been temporary result of some external physical factor. Likewise, whilst the defendant diabetic in *Quick* was held to be a non-insane automaton during the hypoglycaemic attack, a diabetic in *R. v Hennessy* (1989) was held to be insane. In the former the condition was caused by external factors, whilst in the latter, hyperglycaemia was caused by failure to take insulin, stress and anxiety.

Thus the Court of Appeal held that it had arisen, if at all, from internal factors (including the diabetes itself). Finally, in *R. v Burgess* (1991), a man attacked a friend, possibly whilst sleepwalking. Following *Sullivan*, the Court of Appeal held that this amounted to insanity because the cause was internal.

Key Principle

Automatism requires an involuntary act done whilst not conscious of one's actions.

BRATTY V ATTORNEY-GENERAL FOR NORTHERN IRELAND 1963
(see p.149).

Held

❖ (HL) Defendant's appeal dismissed for reasons given below. Lord Denning defined automatism as "an act done by the muscles without any control by the mind ... or an act done by a person who is not conscious of what he is doing ... an involuntary act ...". [1963] A.C. 386.

Commentary

Unlike the defence of insanity which leads to a special verdict, a finding of non-insane automatism leads to an acquittal.

Key Principle

Not every unconscious, involuntary act amounts to non-insane automatism.

BRATTY V ATTORNEY-GENERAL FOR NORTHERN IRELAND 1963
(see p.149).

Held

❖ (HL) Appeal dismissed. The judge was correct not to leave automatism to the jury. The only apparent cause of the defendant's involuntary act was the psychomotor epilepsy (a disease of the mind within the *M'Naghten* rules). Therefore the defence was insanity not automatism. [1963] A.C. 386.

Commentary

(1) Not only do insanity (internal cause, see *Sullivan*) and automatism (external cause, see *Quick*) differ in outcome, they also differ in burden of proof. As stated in *Bratty*, the burden of proving insanity is on the defence but the burden of disproving automatism is on the prosecution. The case also

establishes that where the defence raises automatism, the prosecution (or judge) may introduce insanity.

(2) Involuntary act arising from intoxication is governed by the rules on intoxication and an act is not involuntary just because it is unintended or the result of irresistible impulse: *Bratty*. Examples of non-insane automatism given in the case were: reflex actions, convulsions, lack of consciousness caused by a blow on the head, concussion, and sleepwalking. This last example is now incorrect following *Burgess* (see p.154). A further example of automatism given in *Quick* and *Sullivan* was that of actions occurring whilst recovering from an anaesthetic. Moreover, in *R. v T* (1990), the Crown Court held that automatism might be a defence when post traumatic stress disorder was induced by a rape (an external factor).

Key Principle

Self-induced automatism will not be a defence to a crime of basic intent if the defendant was reckless in becoming an automaton—but it may be a defence to a crime of specific intent.

R. v BAILEY 1983

The defendant was convicted of wounding with intent. He claimed to have been in a state of automatism caused by hypoglycaemia. He appealed against the direction that self-induced automatism was no defence.

Held

❖ (CA) Appeal dismissed. Despite the misdirection, there was no miscarriage of justice. Applying the reasoning from *Majewski*, self-induced automatism could provide a defence to crimes of specific intent. Moreover, not every self-induced automaton would be reckless in the sense envisaged in *Majewski*. It is not common knowledge, even amongst diabetics, that the consequence of failing to eat after taking insulin can be "aggressive, unpredictable and uncontrollable conduct". Therefore, self-induced automatism (arising from factors other than drink or drugs) may be a defence to a basic intent crime unless the prosecution prove that the defendant was reckless in the sense of realising this likely effect of the action or inaction. [1983] 2 All E.R. 503.

Commentary

In *Quick*, the Court of Appeal stated that self-induced or reasonably foreseeable incapacity would not excuse. The court in *Bailey* viewed this as obiter. In any event, *Quick* was decided before *Majewski* and *Bailey* brings the law on self-induced automatism into line with that now applicable to self-induced intoxication (see *Hardie*).

THINK POINT

What sort of problems are caused by the fact that the legal and medical definitions of insanity and non-insane automatism do not correspond? Can you give examples where injustice might be caused by this lack of correspondence?

Can it be argued that detaining a defendant who has been found not guilty by reason of insanity is incompatible with article 5 of the **European Convention on Human Rights?** Reading *Winterwerp v Netherlands* [1979] 2 EHRR 387 might assist you with this point.

Would the outcome differ in a case where the defendant inflicted serious injury on the victim following a bout of voluntary intoxication that caused him to be unaware of what he was doing and a case where a diabetic inflicted serious injury whilst in a hypoglycaemic lack of consciousness caused by taking insulin and not eating.

Defences (2)

14

DURESS

Key Principle
The defendant's will must be overborne by a threat of death or serious personal injury.

> ### R. V VALDERRAMA-VEGA 1985
> The defendant pleaded duress to a charge of importing drugs. The defence was based on his severe financial hardship; threats of injury to himself and his family; and threats to expose his homosexuality. He was convicted on a direction that duress was only a defence if he acted "solely" because of the threats of death or serious injury.

Held
❖ (CA) Defendant's appeal dismissed. Threats of death or serious injury did not have to be the sole cause of the defendant's behaviour but only threats of that nature could amount to duress. In the context of the direction as a whole, the jury had not been misled. [1985] Crim. L.R. 220.

Commentary
The threat need not be against the defendant. As this case illustrates, threats against one's family are also sufficient as also are threats against someone very close to the defendant and, very possibly, threats against those for whose safety the defendant would reasonably regard herself/himself responsible. The latter might include threats against pupils which are issued to a teacher. See further *R. v Hasan* (below).

Key Principle
Execution of the threat must reasonably be believed by the defendant to be imminent and immediate.

> ### R. V HASAN 2005
> (see below)

Commentary

The House of Lords in this case required that the threat be of immediate harm and indicated that any delay between the threat and harm would destroy the defence. "[If] the retribution threatened... is not such as he reasonably expects to follow immediately, or almost immediately, on his failure to comply with the threat, there may be little room for doubt that he could have taken evasive action whether going to the police or in some other way, to avoid committing the crime..." per Lord Bingham. This overrules the decision in *R. v Hudson & Taylor* (1971), where two girls committed perjury, having been threatened with violence if they did not do so. The Court of Appeal allowed their appeal against their conviction and held that as long as the threat was present and immediate at the time of the perjury it did not matter that the injury threatened could not be carried out immediately.

Other cases had required that the threat be of immediate harm and were approved in Hasan, see for example *R. v Cole* (p.159 below)

Key Principle

The defence of duress is excluded when the defendant voluntarily associated with persons engaged in criminal activity in circumstances where the defendant foresaw, or ought reasonably to have foreseen, the risk of being subjected to any compulsion by threats of violence as a result of that association.

R. v Hasan 2005

The defendant was a driver and minder for a woman who was involved in prostitution. The woman's boyfriend, who also acted as her minder, was involved in illegal drugs and had a reputation for violence. The defendant carried out an armed burglary. The defendant said that the woman's boyfriend had threatened him with death or serious injury and had sent another individual to the burglary to ensure that the defendant carried it out and that he brought back the proceeds of the burglary. He was convicted of aggravated burglary.

Held

❖ (HL) Conviction affirmed. The defence of duress was not available if the defendant foresaw, or ought to have foreseen, that as a result of voluntarily associating with criminals, he might be subject to compulsion by threats of violence (whether to commit crimes or not). To deny the defence, it did not have to be shown that the defendant foresaw, or ought to have foreseen, the objective for which duress might be applied to him (e.g. to force him to commit an offence or to commit a particular type of offence). [2005] 2 A.C. 467.

Commentary

Their Lordships reviewed much of the law of duress, observing that duress was easy to plead and difficult for the prosecution to disprove. Accordingly, where policy decisions were to be made, their Lordships were inclined to tighten, rather than loosen, the requirements for the defence.

Key Principle

Duress is only available if the crime committed is one that the defendant was instructed, under threat, to commit.

> ### R. v COLE 1994
> The defendant committed two robberies to repay debts to persons who had threatened him, his girlfriend and their child with violence if the debts were not repaid.

Held

❖ (CA) Defendant's appeal dismissed in respect of duress. The defence was limited to cases where the threatener "nominates" the crime and the moneylenders had not stipulated that the defendant should commit robbery. [1994] Crim. L.R. 582. The appeal must fail also because there had not been an imminent peril.

Commentary

This decision was approved by Lord Bingham in *Hasan*, where he said "[d]uress is available only where the criminal conduct which it is sought to excuse has been directly caused by the threats."

Key Principle

The defendant must respond to the threat as would a sober person of reasonable firmness, sharing the defendant's relevant characteristics.

> ### R. v GRAHAM 1982
> The defendant was convicted of murdering his wife and pleaded duress based on a belief that his lover would kill him if he did not do so. He appealed against the direction that the test for establishing duress was objective.

Held

❖ (CA) Appeal dismissed. Duress provides a defence only if the answer to the two following questions is "Yes": [1982] 1 W.L.R. 294.

1. Was the defendant (or may he have been) impelled to act as he did because, as a result of what he reasonably believed to be the situation, he had good cause to fear that otherwise death or serious injury would result?

2. Are the jury sure that a person of reasonable firmness, sharing the accused's characteristics, would have responded as the accused did?

Commentary

This test is similar to that previously used in provocation under *DPP v Camplin* (1978) (see Ch.6) and was confirmed in *R. v Howe* (1987) (see p.161). Voluntary intoxication is not taken into account in applying the test. Nor is a self-induced drug addiction (*R. v Flatt* (1996)) or low IQ (*R. v Bowen* (1996)), because neither are relevant to the ability to withstand threats. Nor are characteristics such as "unusual pliability or vulnerability to pressure" (*R. v Horne* (1994)) or "emotional instability (and) neurotic states" (*R. v Hegarty* (1994)), since these conflict with the requirement of "reasonable firmness".

Key Principle

Where the defendant mistakenly believes that s/he is under duress or is under duress greater than s/he is in fact under, the defendant can rely upon that mistaken belief only if it was reasonable as well as genuine.

> R. v SAFI 2003
> The defendants pleaded duress to the charge of a number of offences involved in hijacking a plane. They were convicted and appealed against the judge's direction that they could not rely on a mistaken belief that there was an imminent peril.

Held

❖ (CA) Appeal allowed. The test laid down in *Graham* was the correct legal test. There did not need to be a threat in fact. The defendant was entitled to rely upon a belief in the existence of a threat. The jury must judge the defendant on what he reasonably believed to be the situation. [2003] Crim. L.R. 721.

Over the years since *Graham* was decided, several cases in the Court of Appeal had doubted whether it was necessary for a mistaken belief in duress to be reasonably held. This case re-confirmed the test as laid down in *Graham*. In *Hasan*, Lord Bingham reinforced this with the words, "[t]here is no warrant for relaxing the requirement that the defendant's belief must be reasonable as well as genuine." The rule is thus different from the rule which applies to a mistake in the need for self-defence, where a mistaken belief can be relied upon even if it was an unreasonable one: *Beckford* (see p.168).

Key Principle

Duress is no defence to murder.

> R. v HOWE 1987
> The defendant and others were convicted of, inter alia, murder and appealed on three points. One raised the issue of the objective test in duress (referred to above), another raised the issue of liability of accomplices (Ch.12) and another was whether duress was available as a defence to a principal offender to murder.

Held

❖ (HL) Appeal dismissed. Duress was no defence to murder as an accomplice or principal offender. *Lynch* (1975) was overruled and *Abbott* (1977) affirmed. [1987] A.C. 417.

Commentary

According to *Lynch*, duress was a defence for an accomplice to murder but, according to *Abbott* (PC), it was no defence to the principal offender. In *Howe*, the House decided that no rational distinction could be drawn in terms of degrees of participation. The court noted that their decision could lead to anomalies. Not least was the fact that duress might still be a defence to attempted murder and **Offences Against the Person Act 1861** s.18 where the mens rea requirement was satisfied by the same level of blameworthiness as for murder and where the victim's survival could be by coincidence rather than design.

Key Principle

Duress is no defence to attempted murder.

R. v GOTTS 1992
The defendant unsuccessfully raised duress as a defence to attempted murder.

Held
❖ (HL) Appeal dismissed. There was no justification in logic, morals or law for distinguishing between a successful and would-be murderer. [1992] 2 A.C. 412.

Commentary
Whilst the "sanctity of life" could not justify the exclusion of the defence from attempted as opposed to successful murder, the court was swayed by the fact that the mens rea of the offence required more "evil" intent than that for murder.

NECESSITY (DURESS OF CIRCUMSTANCES)

Key Principle
Duress of circumstances may be available as a defence where the defendant's action arises from a fear of death or serious injury.

R. v CONWAY 1989
The defendant claimed that he drove recklessly because he thought that two men approaching his car intended to kill his passenger. He was convicted and appealed on the basis that necessity (acting in an emergency to save his passenger) was a defence.

Held
❖ (CA) Appeal allowed. The defence of necessity (or, as it may be termed, duress of circumstances) is available where the defendant has acted to avoid death or serious injury. It is, however, subject to the same limitations as the defence of duress by threats. [1989] Q.B. 290.

Commentary
This case recognised that duress of circumstances can be a defence. Since the rules are the same as those applicable to duress by threats, a fear of psychological damage, not being a fear of death or serious injury, will not found the defence: *R. v Baker & Wilkins* (1997) (see p.168). Similarly, the defence will fail unless a person of reasonable firmness would have responded as the defendant did: *Martin* (1989) (see p.163).

There must be an imminent and immediate peril or a reasonable belief that there is an imminent and immediate peril to which the defendant responds.

> R. v ABDUL-HUSSAIN 1999
> The defendants hijacked an aeroplane in order to escape death at the hands of the Iraqi authorities. The trial judge ruled that the threat was insufficiently immediate. They were convicted and appealed.

Held ....

❖ (CA) Appeal allowed. Imminent peril of death or serious injury to the defendant or their dependants must be operating to overbear the defendant's will at the time of the offence. The threatened injury need not be immediate. [1999] Crim. L.R. 570.

Commentary ....

This case must now be regarded as wrongly decided, after the emphasis laid by Lord Bingham (in *Hasan*), upon the requirement that the threat must be one which the defendant reasonably believes is liable to be carried out imminently and immediately. For examples where the defence was lost due to lack of immediacy see *R. v Cole* 1994 (p.159), where the link between the peril and the offences was not direct and immediate and *Blake v DPP* (1993) (Ch.10, p.111) where the vicar was denied the defence of duress of circumstances because writing on the pillar was not in response to fear of immediate danger to himself or those with him. Lack of immediacy and imminence of physical injury have also been used to deny the defence of necessity to defendants who have possessed cannabis for the purposes of pain relief. See, for example, *R. v Quayle, Attorney-General's Reference (No.2 of 2004), Re Ditchfield* (2005).

Key Principle ....

The circumstances must be such that a person of reasonable firmness, sharing the defendant's characteristics, would respond as the defendant did.

> R. v MARTIN 1989
> The defendant drove his stepson to work whilst disqualified and pleaded necessity based on a threat from his wife (who had a history of suicidal behaviour) that she would kill herself if he did not do so. He appealed against the direction that necessity was no defence.

Held

❖ (CA) Appeal allowed. The defence was only available if "from an objective standpoint" the defendant acted "reasonably and proportionately" to avoid a threat of death or serious injury. The jury should therefore have decided whether or not a sober person of reasonable firmness, sharing the defendant's characteristics, would have responded similarly. [1989] 1 All E.R. 652.

Commentary

The Court followed *Conway* (above). The test is the same as for the defence of duress by threats. It is also the case that the defendant must desist from the crime as soon as reasonably possible after the peril ceases to be present. Thus in *DPP v Bell* (1992), the defence succeeded where the defendant drove whilst intoxicated in order to escape from a threat of violence because he only drove a short way until a safe distance from his pursuers. Contrast *R. v Tomkinson* (2001), where the defence was lost because the intoxicated defendant drove 72 miles from the danger before being arrested. Also in *R. v Pommell* (1995), it was for the jury to decide whether the defendant, who took possession of a firearm to prevent another from using it, had acted as soon as reasonable in the circumstances when he failed to hand it over to the police immediately.

Key Principle

Necessity is no defence to murder except in highly exceptional circumstances.

> **R. v Dudley & Stephens 1884**
>
> The defendants and victim were shipwrecked on a boat, 1000 miles from land. After nine days without food and seven without water, the defendants killed and ate the victim in order to save themselves. If they had not done so they would probably have died and the victim, being the youngest and weakest, was likely to have died before them. The defendants were charged with murder.

Held

❖ (DC) Conviction affirmed. There was no authority that necessity (other than self-defence) justified a killing. Saving life by killing an innocent and unoffending victim did not fall within the scope of any defence known to the law. [1884] 14 Q.B.D. 273.

The case suggests that it was not in fact necessary to kill the boy. However it appears to go further in holding that it would not, in any event, have been a defence. *Dudley & Stephens* is distinguished in the next case.

> RE A (CHILDREN) (CONJOINED TWINS: MEDICAL TREATMENT) 2000
> Doctors wished to operate to separate conjoined twins, Jodie and Mary. Jodie was capable of independent existence but the operation would kill Mary who was alive only because she was joined to Jodie. Without the operation both twins would die. The judge concluded that the operation would be lawful and the parents appealed.

Held ....

❖ (CA) Appeal dismissed. The operation would be lawful because, per Brooke L.J., "[a]ccording to Sir James Stephen" (*Digest of Criminal Law*, 1887), "there are three necessary requirements for the application of the doctrine of necessity:

  (i)   the act is needed to avoid inevitable and irreparable evil;.
  (ii) no more should be done than is reasonably necessary for the purpose to be achieved; and.
  (iii) the evil inflicted must not be disproportionate to the evil avoided.

... I consider that all three of these requirements are satisfied in this case.".

Commentary ....
Brooke L.J. felt that *Dudley & Stephens* could be distinguished because there was no issue about how to select the victim in this case and because Mary (unlike the cabin boy in Dudley) was a threat to Jodie. His decision is also limited by the fact that the victim was already "designated for death". Walker L.J. dismissed the appeal on other grounds and Ward L.J. limited his decision to cases where doctors had to choose between two conflicting duties towards patients. Therefore it is unlikely that the case provides any general precedent in cases of murder.

SELF-DEFENCE AND PREVENTION OF CRIME

Key Principle ....
A person is entitled to use reasonable force, at common law, in defence of themselves or another and also, under Criminal Law Act 1967 s.3 to prevent a crime or effect an arrest.

Key Principle

Whilst the circumstances giving rise to a plea under s.3 or at common law may differ, they also overlap and the legal requirements for both are similar.

R. V CLEGG 1995

A soldier shot and killed a car passenger and was convicted of murder following an unsuccessful plea of self-defence. The first three shots fired were, he claimed, in defence of himself or a fellow soldier. The fourth shot was fired after the perceived danger had passed and so, if anything, could only fall within the Northern Ireland equivalent of s.3 (force used to effect an arrest). In the circumstances the use of lethal force was excessive and unreasonable. One question on appeal was whether any distinction could be drawn between excessive force used in self-defence and that used in prevention of crime or to effect arrest.

Held

❖ (HL) Defendant's appeal dismissed for reasons given below. It was not practical to distinguish between the defences because of the potential overlap between them. The degree of permissible force and the consequence of using excessive force were the same in each defence, irrespective of whether the defendant is a civilian, a member of the security forces or a police officer. [1995] 1 A.C. 482.

Commentary

Section 76 of the **Criminal Justice and Immigration Act 2008** now also confirms that the same principles apply to both the common law and the s.3 defence. It is not only the concept of reasonable force that is the same for both defences. The effect of the defences and the law relating to mistaken belief in the need to use force is also the same. Moreover, the burden of proof is on the prosecution in respect of the common law defence (*Palmer v R.* (1971) (see p.169) and s.3 (*R. v Kahn* (1995)). *Clegg* also illustrates that reasonable force can be used, at common law, to defend another (and oneself). It may also be used to defend property (for example *Scarlett* (see p.170) and *Attorney-General's Reference (No.2 of 1983)* (1984) (see below)).

Key Principle

For defensive force to be reasonable, it must be necessary to use the force in response to an attack or the fear of an imminent attack.

The defendant was charged with, inter alia, having made an explosive substance (petrol bombs). He was acquitted on the basis of self-defence in that he intended to use the bombs to protect his premises from what he feared to be an imminent attack from rioters and looters.

Held

❖ (CA) The use of reasonable force was not limited to spontaneous reactions on being attacked. It also covered acts done in anticipation of imminent danger and could, therefore, provide a lawful excuse in such cases. [1984] Q.B. 456.

Key Principle

It may still be necessary to use force even though the defendant has not retreated or demonstrated a willingness to disengage before resorting to force.

R. v MCINNES 1971

The defendant stabbed and killed the victim during a fight. He appealed against conviction for murder based on, inter alia, the direction that self-defence is only available if the defendant has done all he reasonably can to retreat before using force.

Held

❖ (CA) Appeal dismissed. Although the direction was too rigid, it had not misled the jury. A failure to retreat is not conclusive, it is simply one factor to take into account in deciding whether or not it was necessary to use force. [1971] 1 W.L.R. 1600.

Commentary

The court approved *R. v Julien* (1969), which stated that there was no duty to retreat but that there was a duty to demonstrate an unwillingness to fight. This latter condition was held to be too stringent in the next case.

R. v BIRD 1985

The defendant was convicted of wounding. Her evidence was that, at the time, she was being held by the victim against a wall and struck back at him in self-defence. She appealed against the direction that it was necessary that she demonstrated an unwillingness to fight before striking.

DEFENCES (2)

Held

❖ (CA) Appeal allowed. Failing to demonstrate willingness to disengage was, like failure to retreat, not conclusive but simply one factor to take into account along with the rest of the evidence. [1985] 2 All E.R. 513.

Commentary

The court agreed that failing to retreat or to offer to withdraw might establish retaliation, revenge or pure aggression rather than self-defence. However, this would not always be the case.

Key Principle

If the defendant genuinely but mistakenly believed that it was necessary to use force, s/he is entitled to be judged on the facts as s/he believed them to be.

BECKFORD V R. 1988

An armed police officer was convicted of murder, having shot and killed the victim. He appealed against the direction that he could only rely on his mistaken belief that he was acting in self-defence if it was based on reasonable grounds.

Held

❖ (PC) Appeal allowed. Following *Williams (Gladstone)* a genuine belief that it was necessary to use force would negate the intent to act unlawfully. Therefore the test for self-defence is whether the force is reasonable in the circumstances as the defendant honestly believed them to be. The belief does not also have to be reasonable. [1988] A.C. 130.

Commentary

(1) The same principle applies to the **Criminal Law Act 1967** s.3: *R. v Baker & Wilkins* (1997). In this case the defendant and her co-defendant were convicted of criminal damage, having broken through a door to gain access to her child who was being hidden by its father. Although the defendants were entitled to be judged on their honest belief, their appeal was dismissed because even so no crime was being committed and so there was no right to use force. Their defence based on the **Criminal Damage Act 1971** s.5(2)(b) (see p.112) and on duress of circumstances (see p.162) also failed.

(2) The position differs if the mistaken belief is caused by intoxication, see *R. v O'Grady* (1987), *R. v O'Connor* (1991) and *R. v Hatton* (2005) in Ch.13.

Key Principle

The degree of force used must be proportionate and no more than necessary in the circumstances.

> **PALMER V R. 1971**
> The defendant was convicted of murder, having shot and killed the victim, in what he claimed to be self-defence.

Held

❖ (PC) Defendant's appeal dismissed for reasons given below. The defence only applied where force was reasonably necessary. This depended on the circumstances of the case but a jury should bear in mind that "a person defending himself cannot weigh to a nicety the exact measure of his necessary defensive action." [1971] A.C. 814.

Commentary

(1) Consider also *McInnes* where the deliberate stabbing was unreasonable in the circumstances and *Clegg* where the use of lethal force against someone not believed to be involved in terrorist activities was "grossly disproportionate to the mischief to be averted". The court in *Palmer* commented that doing what one "honestly and instinctively" thought was necessary was strong evidence that the force used was reasonable. All these aspects of the defence are confirmed in section 76 of the **Criminal Justice and Immigration Act 2008**.

(2) Despite apparent doubts caused by the later case of *Scarlett* (see below), it is clear that the test for the degree of permissible force is objective. This is confirmed in *R. v Martin* (2002) where the defendant shot two burglars, killing one and wounding the other. He suffered from a paranoid personality disorder that caused him to believe he was in extreme peril. The Court of Appeal held that the psychiatric disorder was not relevant in assessing the use of reasonable force in self-defence. This should be contrasted with the decision in *R. v Martin* (2000) and compared with the next key principle.

Key Principle

If the defendant makes a mistake about the circumstances in which force is used, s/he is entitled to be judged on the facts as s/he believed them to be in determining whether, objectively, the force used was reasonable.

R. v SCARLETT 1993

A pub landlord was convicted of constructive manslaughter based on an act of assault. He appealed on the ground that the act causing death was an exercise of reasonable force used to eject a trespasser from the pub.

Held

❖ (CA) Appeal allowed. Even an unreasonable mistaken belief that force used was lawful precluded the mens rea of assault: *Williams* and *Beckford*. Therefore the defendant could only be convicted if the degree of force used was excessive in the circumstances as he honestly believed them to be. [1993] 4 All E.R. 629.

Commentary

(1) The court decided that there was no distinction between mistakes relating to necessity (*Williams* and *Beckford*) and those relating to the degree of force needed (the instant case). Section 76(3) of the **Criminal Justice and Immigration Act 2008** confirms that a defendant is entitled to rely on an unreasonable mistake. This is the case unless it is caused by intoxication: s.75(5) (and see Ch.13).

(2) The decision in *Scarlett* caused consternation because of a suggestion that the test for reasonable force was also subjective (i.e. that the defendant was entitled to use the degree of force that s/he believed was reasonable). However, it is clear that this is not correct. The force used must be objectively reasonable in the light of the facts (including the circumstances and the danger) as the defendant, subjectively, believed them to be: *Shaw (Norman) v R.* (2001).

Key Principle

A successful (or unsuccessful) plea under s.3 or at common law does not mitigate: it is either a complete defence or no defence at all.

R. v CLEGG 1995

(see p.166). The first question raised by the appeal was whether a verdict of manslaughter, rather than murder, was available where self-defence failed because the force used was excessive.

Held

❖ (HL) If the defence succeeds it leads to an acquittal. If it fails it leads to a finding of guilty as charged. Therefore the defendant was guilty of murder because an unsuccessful plea did not mitigate the crime to manslaughter. [1995] 1 A.C. 482.

Commentary

The court expressed the same view that led to convictions for murder in *Palmer* and *McInnes*. Regret was expressed and various recommendations for reform were considered but, ultimately, the House held that any change must be by Parliament and not the courts.

THINK POINT

Do you think that the narrowing of the defence of duress in *R. v Hasan* (2005) (see p.158) is justified? What about the narrow range of characteristics that can be taken into account in applying the objective test, see *R. v Bowen* (1996) (at p.160). Do these conflict with the notion that the defence of duress is a "concession to human frailty": *R. v Howe* (1987)?

Can you explain why a mistake of fact has to be both honest and based on reasonable grounds to be of relevance in cases of duress and necessity and yet it only has to be honest to be relevant in cases of self-defence?

Index

LEGAL TAXONOMY
FROM SWEET & MAXWELL

This index has been prepared using Sweet and Maxwell's Legal Taxonomy. Main index entries conform to keywords provided by the Legal Taxonomy except where references to specific documents or non-standard terms (denoted by quotation marks) have been included. These keywords provide a means of identifying similar concepts in other Sweet & Maxwell publications and online services to which keywords from the Legal Taxonomy have been applied. Readers may find some minor differences between terms used in the text and those which appear in the index.
Suggestions to **taxonomy@sweetandmaxwell.co.uk**.

INDEX